D1015528

More advance praise for
Leadership Step by Step

"Of all the hundreds of leadership books that cross my desk each year, Josh Spodek's *Leadership Step by Step* is by far the most practical. Lots of leadership writers tell stories and relate inspiring examples, and so does Josh. But what makes *Leadership Step by Step* different are the exercises. If you believe, as I do, that leadership is a skill you need to practice and not just an attribute you're endowed with at birth, then you'll immediately see the wisdom in Josh's approach. And if you work his exercises into your own leadership journey, I promise you'll emerge as a better leader."
—Eric Schurenberg, *Inc.* Magazine, Media President and Editor-in-Chief

"The art of leadership, like so many other skills, must be learned 'hands-on' and through experiences, rather than from business-school lectures and abstract analysis. Joshua Spodek has written a great book that takes future leaders through the essential steps of learning to lead. Essential reading for aspiring leaders in any field."
—Tony Wagner, bestselling author of *Creating Innovators* and *The Global Achievement Gap*; Expert-In-Residence at Harvard University's Innovation Lab; Senior Research Fellow at the Learning Policy Institute

"Great leaders aren't born with a 'leadership gene'; great leaders develop the necessary skills and gain confidence through practice and hard work. In *Leadership Step by Step* Joshua Spodek presents a thoughtful approach to becoming a highly effective leader that emphasizes the importance of experiential learning. It will serve as a valuable resource for leaders at all levels in any profession. Indeed, Joshua's practical exercises will help prospective, as well as experienced, leaders to master their craft and ultimately succeed in leading and inspiring others in their various pursuits."
—General Lloyd J. Austin III, U.S. Army, Ret., commanded troops in combat in Iraq and Afghanistan; served as the 33rd Vice Chief of Staff of the Army and 12th commander of U.S. Central Command

"In a fresh approach to the topic, Josh Spodek guides his readers on an experiential journey through a progression of exercises that reveal the inner psychology of leadership and impart critical skills."
—Michael W. Morris, Chavkin-Chang Chair, Professor of Leadership, and founder of the Leadership Lab at Columbia Business School

"There are thousands of leadership books published each year. Most are NOT very helpful. Joshua Spodek's book deserves to break through the clutter. Rather than the usual focus on leadership techniques, this book gets to the holy grail of leading and motivating by helping readers understand themselves and how they affect people."
—Michael Feiner, President of Michael C. Feiner Consulting, author of
The Feiner Points of Leadership; formerly professor at Columbia
Business School; Chief People Officer worldwide at Pepsi-Cola Co.

"Refreshingly different and thoroughly practical, *Leadership Step by Step* serves up valuable tools for readers to build their own path to development. The book weaves back and forth between brief, engaging stories and seemingly simple exercises. But the cumulative effect can be profound, helping readers focus on and sometimes rewrite their habits of thought and action that were previously invisible."
—Daniel Ames, Columbia Business School Professor,
Management Division

"Our nation, and indeed the world, is in desperate need of genuine authentic leadership to solve pressing problems. Using his experience at NYU with instilling passion and dedication into students through active experiential learning, Joshua has created a how-to guide to leadership development. It is a book every educator should read."
—Paul Horn, NYU Senior Vice Provost for Research and Senior Vice
Dean for Strategic Initiatives and Entrepreneurship; formerly Senior
Vice President and Executive Director of Research at IBM, where he
oversaw Deep Blue and helped initiate Watson

"For years acclaimed NYU professor and executive coach Joshua Spodek was frustrated by the existing literature on leadership. Countless fact-filled books described the subject, but not one actually explained how to become a great leader. Now based on years of teaching experience, Spodek has produced the first systematic manual designed to hone great leadership. Filled with personal insights and detailed daily exercises, *Leadership Step by Step* is a vital resource for anyone interested in leading other people."
—David Lefer, Industry Professor and Director of the Innovation and
Technology Forum at the NYU Tandon School of Engineering

"Packed with dozens of thought-provoking exercises that will help you develop the self-awareness and sensitivity to take your leadership game to a new level."
—Caroline Webb, author *How to Have a Good Day;* CEO and founder
of Sevenshift; Senior Advisor and former Partner, McKinsey

"Joshua Spodek has written a very important book distilling universal leadership principles into practical exercises that anyone can do and internalize. Rarely is leadership taught practically, often remaining theoretical and still needing decades of hands-on experience. His practical approach accelerates the process of self-discovery, quickly creating a much more effective mindset and perspective on ourselves and others. My experience in McKinsey, from serving top CEOs to becoming a CEO myself and scaling a global Internet startup with hundreds of employees in four Asian regions, then launching high-achieving teams across Europe, makes obvious the timeless value and universal, underlying principles of Joshua's exercises.Do them seriously and you will significantly improve your personal and professional leadership."

—Jose Gaztelu, Managing Director, Houzz.com; former CEO Zalora
Group Singapore, Hong Kong, Thailand

"Being an effective leader is not just about having a vision, it's about bringing others along with you to achieve that vision. From the very first lesson in *Leadership Step by Step*, this book sets a tone of simple self-exploration that tackles this very challenge—not just through high-level concepts, but through methodical, targeted lessons that are both tactical and results-oriented. This book takes leadership from theory to reality—though to achieve the desired results requires effort, and practice, on the part of the reader. As a student, I was keenly aware that I was getting out exactly what I put into this course. . . . These skills can be (must be) learned and thoughtfully honed. This book is a beautifully crafted guide through that process."

—Bethany Hale, Associate Partner, IBM

"You learn to lead by leading, not just by reading, and *Leadership Step by Step* gives you direction to learn by doing. I've coached thousands of people over the past decade, and the ones who progress are the ones who get off their duff and *act*. If you're willing to work but are struggling to find a starting point, Joshua presents a simple structure of what to do to improve yourself as a leader. Get the book and do the exercises. It really is that simple."

—Jordan Harbinger, cofounder and host, *The Art of Charm*

"Joshua's book clearly articulates the power and value of empathy to not only lead, but motivate. An important fresh look at leadership, because insecurity and anger are powerful but toxic propellants that, unfortunately, many leaders lead with."

—B. Jeffrey Madoff, director, photographer, writer, professor;
and founder and CEO of Madoff Productions,
Webby award winning producer for Victoria's Secret

"Many leadership books leave the reader with more questions than answers. This is book provides not only answers, but actionable insights that can be applied immediately. If you want to become a more effective leader, read this book."

—Srinivas Rao, host and cofounder of *The Unmistakable Creative* podcast and bestselling author of *Unmistakable: Why Only Is Better Than Best* and *The Art of Being Unmistakable*

"*Leadership Step by Step* has you actually DO things, so you learn at the same time you lead people in your life and work. As young entrepreneurs, we hustle. We don't have time to read theory that doesn't connect with what we actually do. We're busy building! We see too many people caught up in analyzing and preparing and not actually making progress. You'll learn faster and deeper with Joshua's book than in any classroom or most other books . . . *and you'll get things done*. If you want to lead real people in real life on real projects, do Joshua's exercises."

—Corianna (Coco) and Brianna (Breezy) Dotson, founders of Coco & Breezy

"*Leadership Step By Step* begins by asking, simply, why don't the world's best leaders come out of the world's top leadership programs? Because the way we teach leadership, it turns out, is out of sync with how people learn, perform, and develop mastery! Joshua Spodek fixes that error, breaking the skill, art, and science of leadership into a series of exercises that guide you to lead people, teams, and yourself beyond what you thought possible. If you want to become a better, more powerful, more empathic, more understanding leader—to take a great leap forward in your leadership journey, both personally and professionally—I could not recommend this book any more highly."

—Zac Hill, Chief Innovation Officer, The Future Project

"With *Leadership Step by Step*, Joshua Spodek has created a thoughtful, practical guide for improving our leadership skills by asking us to think deeply about who we are and how our personal beliefs and actions create our leadership qualities. Spodek doesn't tell us what to think or how to lead, but rather creates a series of thoughtful activities to push us to examine ourselves. At the heart of this book is the idea that to be better leaders, we have to be better people, and this book is a guide for anyone seeking to understand that relationship. It is an important book that can help us all."

—Chris Lehmann, founder of Science Leadership Academy and coauthor of *Building School 2.0: How to Create the Schools We Need*

Leadership

Step *by* Step

Become the Person Others Follow

JOSHUA SPODEK

AMACOM
AMERICAN MANAGEMENT ASSOCIATION
New York • Atlanta • Brussels • Chicago • Mexico City • San Francisco
Shanghai • Tokyo • Toronto • Washington, D.C.

American Management Association: www.amanet.org
This publication is designed to provide accurate and authoritative information in regard to
the subject matter covered. It is sold with the understanding that the publisher is not
engaged in rendering legal, accounting, or other professional service. If legal advice or other
expert assistance is required, the services of a competent professional person should be
sought.

LIBRARY OF CONGRESS CATALOGING-IN-PUBLICATION DATA
Names: Spodek, Joshua, author.
Title: Leadership step by step : become the person others follow / Joshua
    Spodek.
Description: New York City : Amacom Books, [2017]
Identifiers: LCCN 2016042447 (print) | LCCN 2016043531 (ebook) | ISBN
    9780814437933 (hardcover) | ISBN 9780814437940 (eBook)
Subjects: LCSH: Leadership.
Classification: LCC HD57.7 .S697 2017 (print) | LCC HD57.7 (ebook) | DDC
    658.4/092--dc23
LC record available at https://lccn.loc.gov/2016042447

10 9 8 7 6 5 4 3 2 1

Contents

To my past students and clients, from whom I learned so much, and to my future students and clients, who I hope help solve the global problems our world has never faced or had to solve before.

Acknowledgments

If I don't force myself to keep this section short, it will end up as long as the rest of the book. The influence of each person below shows up on every page of this book.

First are my leadership teachers. Despite what I say about the traditional education system they worked in, I learned from them and their courses more than I can say: Daniel Ames, Srikumar Rao, Ralph Biggadike, Michael Feiner, Bill Duggan, and Donald Waite.

Next are my leadership mentors: Marshall Goldsmith, Michael Preston, David Allen, Frances Hesselbein, and Barry Salzberg.

Teachers who taught me that *how* we learn is as important as *what*: Chris Lehmann, Tim Best, Joshua Block, Adam Holman, Bruce McCarty, and Richard Friedberg.

Friends from whom I learned leadership and support: John Emerson, Faron Salisbury, and Sebastian Marshall. Jordan Harbinger and Neil Strauss gave pivotal inspiration in North Korea.

My mom, of course, whose marathon at 67 inspired me as much as anything.

My agent and editor, who saw this book's potential before anyone else: Melissa Kahn and Stephen S. Power. And to my writing partner, Kate Hawley.

A few historical leadership and teacher inspirations stand out enough to mention: Constantin Stanislavsky, Sanford Meisner, James Lipton (whom I hope to meet to tell how much he's inspired me), John Dewey, Aristotle, Laozi, and R. H. Burpee.

Finally, my students and clients, from whom I learned the most about leadership, how to learn it, and how to teach it.

Preface

Have you noticed how many top leaders were once actors, athletes, or other performers? And how few graduated from traditional academic leadership programs?

Actors, athletes, and other performers have become U.S. presidents, governors, senators, congress members, mayors, founders of well-known companies, and more. Love or hate actor-and-athlete-turned-president Ronald Reagan, he ranks near the top of many presidential polls. Meanwhile, the only MBA president, George W. Bush, ranks near the bottom.

Performers-turned-leaders include Arnold Schwarzenegger, Oprah Winfrey, Muhammad Ali, Sean Combs, Jesse Ventura, Jackie Chan, Al Franken, Jane Fonda, and others—not mere trendsetters. Besides not taking traditional leadership programs, many left or failed out of school. By contrast, few politicians or business leaders become performers or athletes.

What's going on? Why do top leadership programs produce few top leaders? Do traditional leadership programs actually produce middle managers? If so, what are our organizations and society losing by relying on them?

More importantly for leadership students and educators, *what works* that we're missing?

Leadership Step by Step is the first book to find what works in other fields and bring together an effective new way to teach and learn leadership beyond the predominant method of lecture, cases, and biography. It leads readers to develop leadership skills, beliefs, and experiences through a comprehensive, integrated progression of exercises that I have tested and refined with hundreds of students at Columbia and New York University (NYU), online, and with private clients. I have also presented at Harvard, Princeton, MIT, INSEAD, and other top schools.

I first learned that schools taught leadership at Columbia Business School, where I got my MBA. Before then, I figured that you were born a leader or you were not. Business school taught me leadership principles, but implementing them after graduation felt like starting from scratch. Trying, say, to negotiate armed with principles but not experience still crippled me with anxiety.

Teaching me *about* leading didn't teach me *to lead*.

After graduating, I consumed leadership books, videos, courses, and any literature I found. They overwhelmingly focused on facts, information, and principles, too, without actionable instruction on how to develop skills and experiences. While facts didn't hurt, what leader became great from knowing more facts? Facts are a commodity that computers handle better.

How performers from other fields led without leadership education remained unexplained.

Two other fields showed me how to teach people to lead. The first was how we teach performers in other fields. The second was experiential, project-based learning—a teaching method tracing its roots to John Dewey and earlier.

How We Teach Performance in Other Fields

Performers in other fields aren't born masters either but learn through disciplined, dedicated, and structured practice. Let's first consider how we *don't* teach performance.

How We Don't Teach Performance

Imagine that piano teachers taught only through lecture, cases, and biography; that piano scales as exercises didn't exist, nor other standard exercises; that everyone learned piano in classrooms at desks listening to lectures on music theory or debating case studies about other pianists; that teachers didn't play but researched and published instead; and that school ended with commencement, meaning that you commenced playing when school ended.

Books on habits of highly effective pianists, 48 laws of piano playing, and pianists' lives would cover principles, not playing. You would write more papers and take more tests than perform. School performances would be for classmates, not the public. You wouldn't face the anxiety of public performance, the exhilaration of nailing a performance, or the shame of blowing one.

You wouldn't expect people to play well by graduation. People who loved playing most would feel frustrated and disengage the most. Those who left or got kicked out might use their freed-up time to practice, developing their voices and learning to enjoy performing while their classroom-bound peers listened to lectures and wrote papers.

How to Teach Performance

Now imagine that someone in that world invented piano scales as an exercise—not just as theoretical concepts—as well as other exercises at all levels.

Then anyone could start playing. Practicing basics develops skills to play actual music. When exercises are based in theory, they teach you theory, too—so it's usable, not abstract. If there are no big jumps in difficulty between the exercises, you can practice your way to mastery.

Lecture-based schools might criticize all that playing for neglecting the theory they consider fundamental. They might not recognize practicing as relevant to learning piano. They might fear their authority diminishing.

Aspiring pianists might rejoice at playing more and learning from it. Some might feel liberated from lecture and analysis. They might create for themselves more opportunities to perform, overcome anxieties, and improve faster. Some might start alternative schools.

We could have imagined fields besides piano transformed from theoretical to practical—dance, sports, singing, improv, and so on. In one case, though, we don't have to imagine. James Lipton, creator and host of *Inside the Actors Studio*, described such a revolution in acting:

> At the end of the nineteenth century, a man named Constantin Stanislavsky rebelled against the kind of presentational hortatory, self-conscious, self-referential, often self-reverential acting that was the norm.
>
> Stanislavsky developed a system of acting and of exercises, of training, of rehearsal, and of performance that went from a theater that was meant to impress to the theater that was meant to express. And suddenly, everything that was external—the fine form, the perfectly articulated vowels, the piercing consonants, the thick make-up, everything that was posed and disbelieved by the actor—god forbid that the actor should cry and mess up his make-up . . . this was the way acting was taught and the way acting was done until the beginning of the twentieth century.
>
> Stanislavsky changed all that. The Moscow Art Theater came to New York and everything changed in America forever. These young people—Stella Adler, Herald Clurman, Lee Strasburg—they went and saw this theater and it wasn't like anything they'd seen before. These people really believed what they were saying.

They were expressing something that was truthful to them and therefore truthful to the audience. It was an extraordinary experience.

It wasn't declaimed. It wasn't recited. It hadn't been rehearsed in front of a mirror. It wasn't perfect.

It was real.

Stanislavsky freed actors from pursuing abstract, inauthentic perfection in favor of exercises that created what felt true and real. His students soon became teachers, creating and refining their styles. Nobody teaches perfection today. Acting didn't abandon rigor or standards, though. Actors today practice with as much diligence and discipline as ever.

It's not surprising for a community that produces genuineness, authenticity, expression, and sensitivity to produce great leaders, even if traditional leadership educators don't get it.

Stanislavsky's system was new to acting, but many fields—dance, voice, improv, and sports, for example—teach through experiential, comprehensive, integrated progressions of exercises, starting with basics. Lecture, theory, and cases have their places, to be sure—after practice.

What do these fields have in common? They are active, social, emotional, expressive, and performance-based (ASEEP). In ASEEP fields, students practice basics until they master them, then progress to intermediates, and so on. Exercises differ between fields, but the structure doesn't. Many results are the same, too: skills, experience, genuineness, authenticity, sensitivity, discipline, vision, expression, and so on.

Leadership is an active, social, experiential, emotional, and performance-based field, too. We teach nearly every ASEEP field through progressions of exercises except leadership. No one has made the leadership equivalent of scales through advanced pieces.

Until this book.

Another Way Not to Teach Performance

Science and the latest findings are another big source of leadership-development literature, exemplified by TED talks, periodicals, and books that summarize and popularize behavioral science. They typically tell an engaging story about an unexpected experimental result that gets you scratching your head, then an alternative, new perspective based on new results, followed by tips for you to use it.

People feel inspired watching and reading this branch of literature, often thinking, "Wow, what an amazing discovery. I can use it to get ahead of other people who don't know it." Few act on the feeling. The pattern is enticing and effective at selling books and event tickets but rarely changes behavior.

Have you noticed that there are no TED talks or "latest findings" literature on how to play piano or basketball? People are just as passionate to improve with them. There is some variation in teaching styles but hardly the relentless and dramatic march of experiment.

Why? First, because practice and rehearsal work, and everyone knows they take time. Nobody suggests, "Learn this one trick and you'll play tennis like a pro." There are tricks, thousands of them, that you learn on the side while learning the basics by practicing and rehearsing.

You can learn tricks unrelated to scales, like playing chopsticks on the piano. They may entertain people at parties, but they don't move you closer to expressing yourself freely, from your heart, to evoke emotions and inspire others. That freedom and ability to express comes through practice, like learning a language.

The difference between chopsticks and scales is that scales are based in theory, which you learn by playing them. Every field has tricks or latest discoveries. They aren't useless, but they're valuable in the long term only to those versed in theory. It's great for dancers to learn flashy flair or spin moves if they've mastered footwork, rhythm, and teamwork. Otherwise, they're cute tricks. Master the basics and you'll pick them up anyway.

Teaching raw theory in ASEEP fields has its place—*after* mastering performance through practice and rehearsal. A responsibility of a teacher is to translate the theory into exercises a student can do and learn from.

The results of practice and rehearsing theory-based exercises with discipline and diligence is fluency, expression, and creativity that come from conforming to the basics of the craft that the latest or hidden findings of a scientific approach may tell you about but cannot create. It's the difference between abstractly knowing a language's rules of grammar and fluently speaking it.

As Martha Graham said,

The dancer is realistic. His craft teaches him to be. Either the foot is pointed or it is not. No amount of dreaming will point it for you. This requires discipline, not drill, not something imposed from without, but discipline imposed by you yourself upon yourself.

Your goal is freedom. But freedom may only be achieved through discipline. In the studio you learn to conform, to submit yourself to the demands of your craft, so that you may finally be free. . . . And when a dancer is at the peak of his power, he has two lovely, powerful, perishable things. One is spontaneity, but it is something arrived at over years and years of training. It is not a mere chance. The other is simplicity, but that also is a different simplicity. It's the state of complete simplicity, costing no less than everything.

Doing this book's exercises will bring you this realism, freedom, power, spontaneity, and simplicity in leadership.

Experiential Project-Based Learning

The second field that influenced *Leadership Step by Step* was experiential, project-based learning. Since this field and its progenitors like Dewey and Montessori are better known, even among lecture-based educators, I'll just summarize its contribution.

Its main influences are prioritizing students' interests over content, engaging students by connecting the material to their lives and interests, learning by doing, drawing classwork from real-world practices, assessing progress with performance rather than testing, and using reflection to reinforce and expand on what they learned by doing.

These practices complement and augment progressions of exercises. Both fields have generations of success. They were waiting for someone to integrate them and apply them to leadership.

Leadership Step by Step

Leadership Step by Step teaches you to lead through what I call ASEEP-style learning:

> A comprehensive, integrated progression of exercises from basics that require no experience to advanced ones that masters can benefit from continuing to practice, with no big jumps between.

I believe that, like Stanislavsky applying his system in acting, ASEEP-style learning will revolutionize leadership training. Instead of giving you answers, it gives you experiences that lead you to discover them for yourself. As one of my NYU graduate students put it,

I like that this course teaches leadership not just by reading theory but actually putting the theory into practice. In most classes we are forced to regurgitate information back to the professor, in this class we are taught to be self-accountable, which is a skill everyone should have. What I learned in this class will stick with me for life. . . . I would recommend this course not just to peers, but anyone interested in leadership. Honestly, even if you don't care about being a leader, this is the kind of class which can help anyone grow as a person, not only bettering themselves in terms of leadership, but also in terms of self actualization. The social skills you learn in this class have never been taught to me in an academic environment.

Although this book starts with basics, the exercises will help leaders and aspirants of all levels, like cardiovascular, balance, or strength exercises in sports—they are valuable for nearly any athlete at any level. Students reported that the exercises were greatly valuable, from undergraduates in their teens to CEOs in their 60s, from those with MBAs and other advanced degrees to those without college degrees, coming from many fields, many countries, and so on.

As Bethany, MBA, an associate partner at IBM who did the exercises in this book online, said,

From the very first lesson, Josh's course sets a tone of simple, self-exploration that felt different from other leadership courses to me because it was so customized to each individual's self-awareness. Each lesson builds on the last and you get out of it exactly what you put in. Each lesson is also very applicable across a wide spectrum of people in a variety of careers because the concepts are so universal. . . . The weekly exercises helped me put my current and long-term work stresses into perspective, because they focused on such small actions. They were bite-sized (in a sense) and weren't overwhelming so they were easy

to fold into my daily routine. Yet, they were extremely impact-
ful.

Instead of preparing you for "real" life after commencement, *Leadership Step by Step* believes your life is real now and that you can
lead now. You will do its exercises with people you care about on
matters you care about. You will face and overcome low-stakes challenges so that when stakes are high, you can act from experience,
not analysis.

To clarify, *Leadership Step by Step*'s exercises come from leadership practice, not acting or other fields, so you learn specific leadership skills while getting general Method Learning results like
genuineness, authenticity, self-awareness, and empathy. Many of
us have taken workshops like improv for leadership, art for leadership, and others. Many work—some tremendously well. They nonetheless have a limitation: If an improv for leadership workshop
goes well, what do you do next? Learn more improv?

Learning leadership from leadership practices means that you
can focus on your practice more. You can keep progressing in the
same field. It also treats leadership like the art it is, in which you
can express yourself fully.

An inspiration and influence was the leadership luminary (and
my mentor) Marshall Goldsmith. His exercises *Feedforward* and *No,
But, However* are leadership equivalents of piano scales. *Feedforward* develops skills in getting advice and building nonjudgmental
relationships. *No, But, However* develops communication skills
while raising self-awareness. *Leadership Step by Step* uses both, and
all the exercises in the book follow their model. They are quick to
learn, are simple (although not necessarily easy), and give value as
long as you practice them. They are based in theory, which they
teach. Marshall crafted them as carefully as any composer did a musical exercise.

Each chapter develops a set of skills, beliefs, and experiences.

Each has three parts—a story illustrating their importance, instructions for an exercise to develop them, and a post-exercise reflection. You learn between the chapters, doing the exercises and then reflecting.

As with any skill, you get out what you put in. As an actor once told me, "You show me the best actor in the room and I'll show you the one who works the hardest." *Leadership Step by Step* enables you to put in as much as you want. Chris, an entrepreneur and salesman who did the book's exercises (and whose interviews you hear before and after each exercise in the online version), described how natural the exercises felt:

> It also helped me start public speaking and very quickly landed my first, second, and third speaking gigs. I now have two-year contracts set up with major corporations all from using what Josh teaches in his leadership course. Again, to an outsider looking in on my progress it seems like it was difficult, the truth is the course exercises instilled in me passive progress that happens naturally. Building up to professional success was as enjoyable as the exercises in his course.

What about getting experience through life? Life also gives you experience, but not comprehensively, nor ordered for your education. Many who face challenges too soon conclude that they can't lead—even if they could have handled the challenges with preparation and then flourished. *Leadership Step by Step* gives you challenges progressively, requiring no experience to start. By the end of the book, you will have practiced and mastered advanced, effective skills that even very experienced leaders don't know.

Readers who don't do the exercises will find *Leadership Step by Step* like any other leadership book—maybe confusing for not just stating facts. Students who want a richer experience can explore the online version available at SpodekAcademy.com, too, which uses the same exercises as the book and the same software as the university courses. The online experience requires students to write and post reflections after each exercise, creating a community of accountability, sharing, and growth.

What You Will Learn

The progression of exercises is structured to take you smoothly from basic to advanced. One of my undergraduate students described the progression this way:

> I found this structure very helpful as it provided us the opportunity to gain practical knowledge instead of textbook knowledge that could be acquired without having to take a course. The class allowed me to learn at my own pace, and really think about what was being taught in class outside of class. . . . I found myself being able to handle situations in team environments with much more effectiveness because I had a reference to the way I was participating in groups. I think Professor Spodek effectively redefined my understanding of leadership and of being a leader . . . He really provided perspective in that we use leadership every day in both encounters with others as well as within myself. Overall . . . an incredibly rewarding course that allowed me to challenge myself to strive for a better version of myself. . . . It required discovering what I wanted to learn through real-life encounters, as opposed to lecture-based classes in which many students only memorize concepts for the exam only to completely forget it in a couple months.

The progression contains four units: **Understanding Yourself**, **Leading Yourself**, **Understanding Others**, and **Leading Others**.

Unit 1: Understanding Yourself focuses on perceptions, beliefs, and thought processes. In this unit, you will develop a foundation of self-awarweness of what you sense, think, and believe, as well as how your mental processes filter and process your world. The rest of the exercises build on this foundation.

Unit 2: Leading Yourself focuses on changing beliefs, changing habits, discovering and speaking your authentic voice, and personal development. In this unit you will start changing how you view the world and see how that change affects you. You'll develop habits in personal and professional development, communication, and attracting people to work with you.

Unit 3: Understanding Others generalizes to others what you learned about yourself in units 1 and 2. You will learn about the human emotional system—what leaders work with. In the process, you will learn how to act on it, including on yours, for more personal development. In this unit you'll start seeing the problems with "leading" through authority, such as how it motivates resentment, and work with more effective alternatives, such as making emotional connections.

Unit 4: Leading Others focuses on leading through empathy, compassion, listening, and supportive management that avoids micromanagement. This unit is the culmination of the exercises. You will learn to behave and communicate to attract others to your teams and then to inspire them to find meaning, value, importance, and purpose in their work. They will want to work effectively, produce quality, feel ownership, and thank you for it.

The results of doing the exercises is that you will develop an integrated leadership practice across all areas of your life—work, friends, family, new acquaintances, and more. Ellen, former founder and CEO of a financial tech startup, describes the effects of these exercises:

> For the past 10 weeks I have been working with my family to deal with placing my 93-year-old mother in a nursing home.
>
> Normally I would have been angry and impatient with my siblings. I would have just grabbed control and charged ahead and probably ruined relationships with them forever. Instead, I was able to manage my feelings, see what was going on for them emotionally, and manage to the situation with the goal in mind. We moved my mother on Wednesday and it was amazing on so many levels. Joe, my husband, kept saying that I have been "transformed," he kept saying I don't know how you do this without wanting to kill everyone. My brother for the first time ever said I was wonderful and he was grateful. He thanked me. Most bizarre of all was that I really enjoyed working with my mother and my brother and husband. It was a joy!
>
> And this was all going on as I started two consulting jobs. Not only am I having fun, but I think these may turn into full time jobs—can you imagine, I'm 66 and may have a real job leading the build-out of a new company.

Understanding Yourself

Unit 1: Understanding Yourself focuses on perception, beliefs, and thought processes. In this unit you will develop a foundation of self-awareness of what you sense, think, and believe, as well as how your mental processes filter and shape your world. The rest of the exercises build on this foundation.

CHAPTER 1

The Personal Essay

I had met Frances Hesselbein when she spoke to my leadership class in business school but hadn't gotten to know her.

Frances rose from being a local Girl Scouts volunteer to serving as CEO of the national organization for 14 years. Turning the Girl Scouts around, among other achievements, won her the Presidential Medal of Freedom, 21 honorary doctorates, and more. She's now the president and CEO of the Frances Hesselbein Leadership Institute (renamed in her honor from the Peter F. Drucker Foundation for Nonprofit Management). In short, I could learn a lot from her.

As it happened, I got my chance while writing this book, a decade after she spoke to my class. I reintroduced myself to her at Marshall Goldsmith's book launch. He's my mentor. She is his. We chatted, and she invited me for coffee at her Park Avenue office. Of course I accepted. To call the place impressive would understate what you see there: Her books translated into dozens of languages are framed on the tops of each wall. Below them are photographs of her with U.S. presidents, many-starred generals, and heads of industry. Around eye level are military swords glinting in the sun above framed notes from the dignitaries who gave them to her.

She sat me on her couch. An assistant set up her chair beside me, putting maybe two feet away a woman whom great leaders have called the best leader they've met. The chat I expected could have felt heavy, even intimidating. Her friendly, disarming smile masked the challenge of what she asked when she sat and looked me in the eye: "So, what do you want to talk about?"

I felt like it was a command performance and I was onstage. What do you say when one of the world's great leaders asks you to lead?

I had wondered this question for weeks, since she had invited me. Our only interaction between her business school talk and the book launch was online, when she tweeted about a blog post of mine—a pleasant surprise. I couldn't imagine how she found it. Six months later, I saw her at the book launch. We spoke briefly. (Me: "How did you know to tweet about my post?" Her: "Oh, yes, I have a girl who does that.") She lived up to her gracious reputation, emptying her purse on a library table to find me her business card. People must have wondered who the young man getting her attention was.

I accepted the invitation for coffee enthusiastically. Only when preparing to go did I think about what to say—not so easy with a Presidential Medal of Freedom honoree. My first thought was to ask for tips on leading, but I didn't want to waste her time with what I could read in her books. What could I talk about when I barely knew her? Then I remembered, "Wait a minute. *I teach this!*"

My leadership course includes teaching how to make meaningful connections. I call the exercise, which is in this book, *Meaningful Connection*. I've taught and practiced it for years, maybe not with people who hang out in the White House, but I still knew what to do.

That's the value of technique. You can fall back on it when you don't know what to do, which calmed me—even in the high-ceilinged marble lobby when the guard reinforced her status: "Frances? Yeah, she's big. Four-star generals wait for her. General Shinseki waited over there."

If I did not have a technique, her question in that office would have made me nervous. Instead, I knew what to say. "I feel like leadership is a passion of yours," I began, leading into the exercise. The conversation lasted over two hours—well beyond the originally scheduled 30 minutes. She took me to lunch, where everyone treated her with reverence. We talked about leadership; service; passion; teaching; the "hallowed ground" of West Point, where she teaches and speaks regularly; and her friendship with Alan Mullaly, the former CEO of Ford. Eventually, her assistant interrupted us to insist we finish because her next appointment was waiting.

"I don't remember a more delightful conversation," she said as we wrapped up. She was fascinating, insightful, charming, and generous. Not only did she answer in few words questions that I had pondered for years—that's the value of experience—but she invited me to West Point; referred me to a retired general who ran one of its leadership programs; and referred me to the editor of her institute's journal, *Leader to Leader*. The technique worked. I knew what to say and how to behave to make the opportunity enjoyable and productive for both of us.

A decade before, such an interaction would have paralyzed me with anxiety.

In fact, one did, eight years earlier. The author of a book I liked was speaking at a panel near me. Business school had instilled in me the imperative to network, so I felt compelled to use the opportunity to meet him. I attended and worked up the nerve to approach him after he spoke.

I said, "Hi, my name is Josh. I wanted to tell you that your book meant a lot to me and I wanted to thank you for writing it."

"Thank you," he replied.

My mind then raced to find something to say—anything—but came up with nothing. We stared at each other awkwardly for 10 or 15 seconds that felt like a year.

Needing to end the discomfort, I said, "Well, great to meet you," and walked away. I didn't get anything out of the conversation, and he probably thought I was weird.

I had taken leadership courses at a top business school, but learning *about* leadership didn't mean learning to *lead*. For all the theory the school taught, I didn't have the skills or experience to handle my emotions or inner monologue. How many connections had I missed or flubbed?

What changed between my anxious failure with the author and confident success with Frances?

Three things. First, relevant experience. I lived the experience that the exercises in this book will give you. I learned what works and how to do it, not just to talk about it.

Second, I led hundreds of clients and students through the exercises online at NYU, Columbia Business School, and private firms. I developed the leadership equivalent of piano scales so you can reproduce my results in months instead of years and without wasted effort. All of that teaching and coaching reinforced what I learned, which gave me more experience and confidence.

Third, I learned to create opportunity and to enjoy relationships with the people I met, not for their status or what they could do for me. I learned to enjoy myself while getting more done with less effort. I'd become more resolute, deliberate, and disciplined.

My editor will say, "Josh, don't tell them *about* these changes in your life. Show them through stories." This book does more—what no leadership book I know does. It will lead you through the same transformations. So you'll meet your equivalents of White House honorees; know what to say to them; and develop your confidence, authentic voice, and ways to inspire.

The *Personal Essay* Exercise

Acting without direction can lead you to work hard and go nowhere, so let's start with direction.

What to Do

The first exercise is to write a personal essay on leadership and why you decided to follow this course of exercises. The personal essay has three goals:

1. To lead you to reflect on yourself and leadership
2. To direct and clarify your focus for the course
3. To record your perspective to hold yourself accountable to it

I recommend writing 500 to 1,000 words, but write as much as you like. Show it to others or not as you like, although the more you share, the more people can connect with you and help if you're open to it. Perhaps most importantly, sharing gives you accountability to someone else.

To help focus you, at the end of your essay, I recommend writing a message explaining the value of taking a Method Learning course on leadership. I suggest a few sentences beginning with "Doing a course of exercises like this is valuable because . . ."

You can write about what you want, but some questions and topics to consider include:

- What motivated you to do this book's exercises?
- What do you expect to gain from the experience?
- What motivated you to pursue leading in general?
- What do you think about leadership?
- What are your models for leadership?
- Who are your role models?
- What works for you when you lead? What doesn't?
- Where do you want to apply your leadership skills?
- What is your history with leadership—first memories, best and worst memories, and so on?
- What is the value in doing these exercises?

After writing your essay, I recommend sleeping on it, rereading it, and editing it. Even if you don't plan to show it to anyone else, the process leads you to reflect.

Now it's time to resist the urge to continue reading and to start your first exercise. Some relevant words on introspection and leadership from Isabeaux, an undergraduate who took my course:

> To be honest, I was initially frustrated with the class, but as a couple classes passed by, and alongside many of the exercises Josh had us undergo, I was able to realize that my "frustration," was in fact my body reacting to being placed outside of its comfort zone. Usually whenever I am bothered or irritated by something, it is actually addressing something within me that I am either neglecting or denying. Josh's course and homework was synonymous with my daily and personal life—a rare experience in a traditional academic setting. . . . His exercises forced me to think extremely introspectively about my life—leading me to change many previous staunch and unnecessary beliefs I held.

EXERCISE CHECKLIST

I recommend checking off the following before continuing:
- ❏ Did you reread your essay, sleep on it, and edit it?
- ❏ Did you consider sharing it with anyone? If so, did you?

Post-Exercise

Congratulations on finishing the first exercise!

I hope you found it simple and that it helped focus your thoughts on leadership and yourself. If it seemed too simple, don't worry, things will pick up soon. You'll use this benchmark over the course to help measure and direct your work.

CHAPTER 2

Perception, Focus, and Attention

Most people would envy Greg's life. He's a former coaching client and the CFO of a major media company in New York City. He graduated from Stanford as an undergraduate and got an MBA from Columbia.

He has a loving and supportive wife and a teenage son with good grades. When we met, he was in his mid-50s, still rising in his already successful career.

In our first call, he told me his immediate reason for coaching: his CEO. He told me that he and most of his coworkers were frustrated with the CEO's leadership, but his strong relationships with the board and investors meant he wasn't going anywhere. The company was also close to an exit, so many employees, including Greg, felt motivated to stay for the likely cash payout, although how much longer, no one knew. As a separate issue, he told me that he considered himself too quick to anger and wanted to learn to handle his emotions more effectively.

Greg's longer-term reason for coaching was the second-most powerful thing I heard him say:

> If I continue on this path, in 10 years I'm going to retire rich, successful, and with no idea what my life was about.

Despite succeeding in every measurable aspect of life and having access to every resource our society offers, he couldn't figure out what it all meant.

I suggested that material and external resources may not have been what was missing—which he knew anyway—but that new experiences could teach him what reading, listening, and other passive learning couldn't. He had to *experience* that meaning, value, importance, purpose, and self-awareness arose from motivations, relationships, and emotions, not the intellect. I think it helped him to hear that he could develop empathy, compassion, intuition, and similar qualities from someone with as analytical a background as a Ph.D. in the abstract field of physics. If someone like that could get this stuff, so could he.

He told me that he would talk it over with his wife before signing on. By the next week, they had talked, she had agreed, and we started.

We began by focusing on his relationship with his CEO with exercises in this book on perception, focus, and awareness. He made significant progress. For example, although he couldn't change much of the CEO's behavior, he learned to manage how he responded. He began to live it. He became more calm at work, he told me, and less reactive to his CEO. Colleagues saw the change and started reporting unofficially to him instead of the CEO. Board members and investors met with him more. He kept the CEO in the loop, avoiding surprises or other relationship problems.

A little over six months into our work, Greg told me about a conversation at home:

My wife, son, and I were talking after dinner. Something came up. The details aren't important, but I could see why it would annoy my son. But he didn't just get annoyed. He flew off the handle. I mean really angry.

I said, "Son, what's gotten into you? I can see why you would be annoyed, but there's no reason to get this angry."

And he said, *"But, Daddy, that's what you would do."*

Greg paused. Maybe he was just collecting his thoughts, but the effect was to make his son's words repeat in my mind: *But Daddy, that's what you would do.*

He continued,

Josh, I can discipline my boy for misbehaving, but not for emulating his father. And the thing is, for all I know he's behaved and said things like this before. I just don't know. I never noticed.

That was the most powerful thing I heard him say.

No parent wants a legacy like an angry son. Greg loved the boy and gave him the best life he could, but his lack of awareness was undermining his effort. Coaching awoke him to what his eyes and ears sensed but his mind didn't process because his focus and attention were elsewhere. He told me how questions flooded his mind: How many times had he reacted with too much anger in front of his son? What else had he taught his son without realizing? What else had he missed his son saying? Could he change? If so, how?

We all do what Greg did. We have goals and try to ignore distractions. Focus helps us achieve the goal, but it doesn't give us *extra* attention. We sacrifice it elsewhere, usually unknowingly, precisely because we aren't paying attention to where we sacrifice it. Learning about focus, attention, and perception in the abstract doesn't translate to improving your focus, attention, or perception any more than learning about the piano in the abstract helps you play music. You only experience what you miss when you focus your attention back there, even your relationship with your son.

Seeing what he was missing led us to work on it and awoke Greg to areas of his life that he had unconsciously made "elsewhere"—family in particular and relationships in general. He also felt the difference between learning abstractly versus through experience. He had known *abstractly* to pay attention to his son before the incident. He didn't know how to do it.

Soon after, instead of asking or wondering what his life was about, he told me.

The *Three Raisins* Exercise

Every leader I've heard say anything about self-awareness describes it as fundamental to leadership and growth. Every system of leadership, professional development, or personal development I've seen has some concept of self-awareness at its foundation. Yet most people don't know what it means—those who lack it most more than anyone.

Talking, reading, or being lectured about self-awareness doesn't help you increase it. Experience does. We'll start with an exercise in awareness of our senses, which later exercises will extend to awareness of other parts of ourselves. This chapter's exercise starts you off more effectively than any other I know. It comes from one of the premier figures in mindfulness today, Jon Kabat-Zinn's book *Coming to Our Senses*. Many who finished this book's exercises consider it the cornerstone, as do I.

When I teach the course in person and assign the exercise, I ask my students if it sounds odd. Many say yes. The next week, after they've done it, I ask if I should assign it the next year even if it seemed weird when they heard it. They always say yes.

It will also introduce many of you to the value of Method Learning—that is, you'll find yourself learning things doing the exercises that you never could from someone telling you.

What to Do

1. Get three raisins. You can use raisin-sized pieces of other fruit if you prefer.

2. Block off an hour when you can turn off your phone and other distractions. You won't take that long, but the cushion keeps you from feeling rushed.

3. During that hour, put the three raisins in front of you and eat them as follows:

- Imagine you've never seen one before.
- Observe it with all your senses in turn. Look at it—its folds, its color, and so on. Feel it in your fingers, how it moves when you press on it. Try to detect if it has a smell. Taste it before you bite into it and then after. Feel how it dissolves in your mouth. Hear its sound if you drop it on a plate. And so on with all your senses.
- Only start the next raisin after you have swallowed all of the remnants of the first.

4. If your attention drifts from the raisins, return your focus to your sensory experience of the raisins.

EXERCISE CHECKLIST

I recommend checking off the following before continuing:
- ❑ Did you use the attention and focus of all of your senses?
- ❑ Did you finish each raisin before starting the next?
- ❑ Did you reflect on the experience?

Stop reading. Put the book down and do the exercise.

You can't build muscle by reading about lifting weights, nor learn to sing by reading about singing, and no leader became great just reading about leadership.

Students consistently learn leadership from doing these exercises. You'll remember the experiences long after you forget what you read. Students consistently say, "These exercises are challenging, but just the challenge I needed to learn from them."

REFLECTION QUESTIONS

Before continuing to the post-exercise section, I recommend reflecting on your experience with this chapter's exercise. Students who take my courses have to write reflections to get to the next exercise and often describe writing their reflections as among the most valuable part of the course.

Write about anything you found relevant, but here are some questions you may want to consider:

- What is the value of seeing your son's or other loved one's expressions?
- Who notices if you miss them?
- What about the nuances of your boss's communications?
- What can you do if you sense them?
- What did you observe about your senses and attention?
- What did you observe about your ability to focus?
- Where and how might you apply your experience in the rest of your life?

Post-Exercise

I hope you found the three raisins experience as revealing as I did.

When I first did the exercise, more than ten years ago, I expected it to take a few minutes. I took at least thirty. From the moment I picked up the first raisin to look at it and noticed the detail in the folds of its skin and its iridescence, I was amazed at how much detail there was to sense. Without going into thirty minutes of that detail, I noticed things I hadn't paid attention to since maybe my first time eating a raisin: its flavor (or rather its mix of flavors—sweetness, tangyness, and hints of others—that rose and fell in turn), its juiciness despite being dried, how the juice burst into my mouth, and so on. I felt like I was eating a raisin for the first time in decades, as if with all the raisins I had eaten in the meantime, I wasn't eating raisins so much as going through motions.

The flavors, smells, and other sensory properties *had* always been there. When I examined my mental processing like I examined the raisins, I saw that I *had* sensed them, I just didn't pay attention, so what I sensed didn't make it to my conscious awareness. I then started noticing other things during the exercise: the sounds of my apartment building, like people coming and going or dogs' paws pattering on neighbors' floors, wind on the window screens, traffic outside, and my breathing.

I started wondering how the raisins got to the box on the shelf in the store—picked from a vine, processed, packaged, and shipped by who knows how many people organized in who knows how many companies, working among the many systems that make up the modern world.

I almost put the second raisin in my mouth while I was still chewing the first, not close to having swallowed all the bits still in my mouth, showing how large parts of my behavior went on auto-pilot like my senses. I value not having to pay attention to how I do every little thing—walking or talking would be impossible otherwise—but I was surprised at how much I glossed over without realizing it.

The experience also highlighted that I had the ability to choose to focus on what I wanted when I wanted, like a skill I could develop.

Beyond the experience with the raisins, after I finished, I returned to a plate of spaghetti I had planned to eat after the raisins, now cold since I thought the exercise would take five minutes. I twirled a forkful as usual, but couldn't put it in my mouth. In my mindset of tasting nuances and subtle flavors and textures, the amount I put on my fork looked gross—in two senses: large and yucky. The volume of food on my plate looked gross too. I couldn't help but change how I ate that spaghetti to like how I ate the raisins, leaving much of it for leftovers. From that exercise for the rest of my life, I have put less food on my plate, focusing more on subtlety and nuance in flavors, smells, textures, and such. I favor fruits and vegetables over pastas and filler. The exercise led to a major shift to eating being about joy and pleasure in sensing and away from just swallowing. The former leads to discovery, refinement, and appreciation. The latter led me just to eat more, with less appreciation or joy.

Many people like that during the exercise they noticed the raisin flavor for the first time since the first raisin they tasted, decades before. The taste was always there, they realize. They just stopped noticing it. Many connect the raisins to other parts of life, like how the raisins got from the vine to the store or how we evolved to like the flavor so much.

Many wonder, if they desensitized themselves to something so obvious, what else they've missed, as Greg did with his son. Did they not notice relationships? Facial expressions? Things people said?

I wish assigning an exercise to observe your son—or manager, spouse, parents, or anyone else—as if for the first time would get people to see other people anew as so many do with the raisins. It seems we learn the skills to pay attention and focus by starting with simpler things, like raisins. Eventually we learn to see abstract things like jobs and relationships anew and more directly.

I assign the exercise at the beginning for a few reasons. One is to underscore how everything we know about our worlds comes through our senses but that we become desensitized to miss many things, from a raisin's taste and other sensory properties to a son's behavior.

Another reason is to call attention to the importance of experience in the exercises to come. No one can tell you how a raisin tastes, nor what you notice when you focus on it for the first time in years, nor how you might generalize your experience noticing things about raisins to noticing things about yourself, other people, and so on. If you're reading this without having done the exercise, you're missing out on the value of doing it. If so, I recommend going back and doing it!"

Another reason is to uncover your ability to focus your attention to make the skill available to you for the exercises to come. When you're leading others, noticing their facial expressions, tone of voice, and other parts of nonverbal communication will make the exercises more effective on a scale I couldn't describe but the raisins can illustrate. The same goes for the next exercises in mindfulness, to focus your attention to sense your thoughts and emotions.

The lessons from this exercise still help me almost daily, 10 years after first doing it. I pay more attention to my food, which I enjoy and appreciate more, eating less while feeling more satisfied. More generally, it helped me develop skill to pay more attention to my senses when I want, deliberately, and to realize what I'm missing when I don't.

The exercise didn't give me *more* attention. It made me more skilled in directing and focusing it. We'll use this skill in most of the rest of the course, especially in chapter 3's exercise, where we pay attention to our thoughts.

I found that when I didn't sense nuances in my food, I had to get my eating pleasure from eating more. Or rather, when I learned to sense subtlety, blindly and tastelessly eating more felt gross. This exercise led me to see that pattern everywhere. What do you know about people, the world, or anything except through your senses? What do you know about if your access is only through gross generalizations?

Choosing to focus on things such as my work, relationships, and eating led me to find meaning, value, importance, and purpose (MVIP) in their richness and complexity, like a fine wine. I hope you get similar results. To see them takes time. For now, you can find them experiencing this book's exercises and the reactions they create in the people and projects you apply them to.

CHAPTER 3

Inner Monologue

Beth and I caught up as we meandered among the paintings and sculptures on display. She was telling me about leaving the multinational corporation where she'd worked for nearly a decade since we graduated. She wanted to start something entrepreneurial.

"Oh my God!" she interrupted herself, her eyes suddenly wide open, fixed on some people about 20 yards away. "Do you know who that is?" she asked.

"Who?" I asked, not clear whom she meant. I didn't recognize anyone.

Pointing, she said, "That woman is the person I want to meet more than anyone else in the world," now more like a teenager seeing a crush, not knowing what to do.

To see someone impressive there wasn't surprising. We were at the VIP preopening of the Armory Show, New York City's premier annual art fair, named for the 1913 Armory Show that introduced impressionism and cubism to the American public. The exhibitors are the most prestigious galleries around the world. They show their top pieces to collectors, curators, and art-world professionals before the show opens to the public on the weekend.

In attendance were celebrities, financiers, and other influential types. Valets parked Ferraris and Bentleys outside. Normally snobby gallery owners had to treat everyone graciously since anyone could be a buyer. Since everyone had status, everyone was approachable.

Beth's background gave her reason to be confident. She had Ivy League degrees in business and law as well as the near decade of high-level corporate experience. Nonetheless, seeing this woman made her nervous.

Beth told me who the woman was—a major player in the venture capital and entrepreneurial world. She and her husband were both well-known investors. Beth had followed her for years while dreaming of the move toward entrepreneurship she was just telling me about, and here was her dream contact. Great! Except she didn't know what to say.

Beth's eyes fixed on the woman, as if she saw a celebrity. Then they darted around, apparently looking for clues about what to do from everyone else. The best option seemed to me to say hello, but Beth didn't move. Actually, she did—in the opposite direction, behind me. Meanwhile, the woman didn't know we existed.

Frankly, I also felt anxious from considering how this woman could help me too. I wanted Beth to approach her so I could meet her, too. "Why don't you go up to her and introduce yourself?" I asked.

"I don't know what to say," Beth said. "Besides," she added, "I can't talk to her *here*."

We both knew that was a red herring because the VIP context equalized everyone. Still, who hasn't frozen in the face of an unexpected opportunity? I had, a few years earlier with the author after the panel.

"You can if you want to. You can say hi."

"How can I just *say* that? I don't know what to say."

Had I asked, I expect she would have said that her mind was blank. Students, coaching clients, and friends report feeling blank when confronted with talking to people they considered having higher status. So did I until I learned to handle my thoughts better. Her mind was more likely the opposite of blank, probably saying things more like this:

> Oh my God, that's her! I've wanted to meet her for so long and now she's actually here. . . . I can talk to her. . . . But what will I say? If things go well she could make me her protégé. I could work with her. My dreams will come true! This is my chance! Oh, but what if I say something wrong? Oh my God, what if I ruin it? If I mess things up she might think I'm weird or not worth working with. . . . I might lose my chance with her. She might never work with me. Maybe I should just wait. Yeah, that's it. If I don't approach her this time, I can think of this occasion as familiarizing myself with her. Then next time I'll be better prepared. And I'll tell her I saw her here so she'll know me. But then I sound like a stalker. Maybe that's worse. And Josh is telling me just to say hi. Like it's that easy! Maybe it is that easy! Beth, don't be such a baby. Just go talk to her! But what do I say? I can't just say hi. . . . I mean, I can, but what would I say next? I'm such a loser. If I can't just say hi to someone, how can I expect to succeed? Why don't I just say hi? Beth, you can do this. No, better just to wait for next time. Yeah, next time will go great. But I've wanted to meet her for so long and now she's actually here. . . . I can talk to her. . . . But what will I say?

Sound familiar? While only Beth knows her exact inner monologue, I've experienced enough similar situations in my life and with clients to guess that it was close. Many people laugh at reading or hearing aloud for the first time something they've always heard in their heads, no longer having to keep a vulnerability secret.

I offered to talk to the woman first and break the ice. Beth protested and then reluctantly agreed. Since I had similar anxious thoughts, I consciously chose to put another thought into my inner monologue that works for me in networking situations: "She seems interesting. I wonder what she's like." I walked over and introduced myself. She turned out to be pleasant and happy to talk. She even asked, "I know you from somewhere, don't I?" I was sure that she didn't, but it made the conversation friendly. I took that moment to introduce Beth.

Beth began telling the woman about being a fan and following her writing for years. They found a lot to talk about, got friendly fast, and took over the conversation.

Like me with the author on the panel, despite her top-tier MBA leadership classes, Beth knew *what* to do but not *how* to lead someone she didn't know. When it counted, anxious self-talk drowned her ability to plan and act. Schools teach that self-awareness is important, if they teach about it at all, but don't give you *experience* or *skills* managing or using it. Skills and experience don't come from lecture or case study.

Our inner monologues run through our minds nonstop. You may notice it in your mind now, maybe thinking something like, "Really? Do I have words running in my head right now? Oh, that's weird, I do. I'm thinking the words that I'm reading."

Although our inner monologue filters, interprets, and gives meaning to our worlds—even when it dominates our minds to the point of paralysis, as it did with Beth—we rarely consciously notice it.

The *Write Your Inner Monologue* Exercise

Awareness of our inner monologue liberates us from it unconsciously controlling us and enables us to use it to improve our lives.

From Your Senses to Your Thoughts

This exercise shifts our attention from our senses to our inner monologue (people also call it self-talk, mental chatter, inner voice, voice of judgment, and so on). People tend not to notice theirs despite its presence nearly every waking moment, like fish not knowing they're in water.

This exercise makes us aware of it. Future exercises will develop skills to use it, which we'll see as critical in leading others and ourselves, but we'll start with awareness.

Our inner monologue chatters incessantly, but we rarely pay attention to it. Many of us have never noticed it consciously. When we do, we can learn a lot. This exercise reveals more about it more effectively than any other technique I know. I learned it from one of my leadership professors, Srikumar Rao, and his book, *Are You Ready To Succeed?*.

You may notice some things about it already. It uses regular language, unlike some mental activity. One part of your mind thinks it while a different part observes it. It takes cues from your environment but can jump on its own from topic to topic. It often evaluates and judges.

Comparing your inner monologue with how you might answer "What are you thinking?" helps clarify it. A typical answer like "I'm thinking about what to eat" is what you're thinking *about* rather than what you're thinking. Your inner monologue is what you're thinking at the word level. It goes more like this:

I'm hungry. . . . wonder what I'll eat. Is it 12:30 yet? Oh no, it's only noon, it's too early to eat now. . . but I'm hungry. . . . Man, I've been eating too much lately. . . If I make it another half hour I'll be good. I'm so bad at controlling my diet. . . . I'd better work out after work today. . . That'll be good, I'll work out. . . Then I can eat early. What time is it now . . . ?

Like breathing, you can consciously control it, but if you don't, it will run on its own. Unlike breathing, your unchecked inner monologue may go all over the place with no prompting.

What to Do

1. Carry a notebook or paper and something to write with every day during the exercise. (You can use your phone, tablet, or computer if you're more used to it.)
2. A few times each day, write the words of your inner monologue as best you can, a few lines each time. What you write will look like the examples in this chapter.

Each time you write will probably take about a minute. Do the exercise until you write a few dozen passages (more is fine), taking maybe an hour cumulatively. I recommend doing it at least for several days so that you record your thoughts in different situations— at work, at home, alone, with people, feeling different emotions, and so on—to see how your inner monologue changes with context.

Record your thoughs without judgment. You will likely find not judging hard, but the goal is to raise awareness, which judgment clouds. If you find your thoughts putting someone down, making yourself feel good or bad, distracting you, or anything else you like or don't like, just write the words in your monologue. Later exercises will work on meaning.

What to Expect

You can't write as fast as you think, so at first writing your thoughts will feel like drinking from a fire hose. Also, writing affects your thoughts, so you have to learn to capture a thought, remember it, and record it independently of what you're thinking while writing.

Note that your mind is never blank. If you think it is, it's likely saying something like,

> I can't think of what I'm thinking. My mind is blank. How do I write anything down? I don't understand this exercise. How am I supposed to write what I'm thinking when I'm not thinking anything? This doesn't make sense. . . .

Or, in another context where people often feel like their mind is blank:

> I wish I knew what to say. I should just go up and talk to him. But I always say the wrong thing. If only I knew what to say. Now I waited too long. They'll probably think I'm weird after not saying anything for so long. Just go say something. Nobody else is talking to him. God, I'm so pathetic.

Examples

You might write something like this if you wrote your inner monologue entering a social situation. (You don't have to write this much each time.)

> I've finally gotten here. I hope I'm not late. Wow, a lot of people here. I wish I were walking in with someone instead of by myself. Now maybe people think I don't know anyone. I don't want them thinking I don't know anyone. Then I have to meet people

from scratch. That's so hard. And I have to cover the same old boring "so what do you do, where are you from, blah blah blah. . . . " Hey, is that Jim? If it's Jim I can say hi to him right away and everyone will know I know him. . . . Darn, no, it looked like Jim, but it's not. I should look for Mary. She's hosting this so she'll know a lot of people and can introduce me. I wonder who else is here. . . . Those guys over there look like they're having fun. I wish I were with a group. Then I'd have fun, too, instead of being by myself and wishing I was having fun. Oh, no, that guy over there doesn't have anyone to talk to either and he looks like he might approach me. I don't want to talk to some guy by himself. What am I saying? I'm by myself. I'm not better than him. I'd better find some people to talk to quick so I'm not stuck by myself. Should I talk to them? I don't want to seem too eager. . . .

Later you might write something like this:

This wine is good. I wish there were more food. I wonder how long I have to talk to Don here. He's interesting but I don't feel like talking to him any longer. But I don't have anyone else to talk to and I don't want to walk around on my own. Nor do I want to start conversations from scratch. Hey, who just walked in the room? She's attractive. I like her dress. She looks good in it. I wish I could look so good myself. She probably had plastic surgery. . . . Was that mean? I wish I didn't think such mean things. I wonder if I can talk to her? Oh wait, she came in with someone just behind her. Darn, she's probably busy. I wonder who that guy is. Oh wait, someone else is coming in behind her. I wonder if I know them. I wish someone came in that I really liked so I could have a great time. Instead I have to talk to Don . . . and that woman who walked in is already talking to someone. I wish I were too. . . .

EXERCISE CHECKLIST

I recommend checking off the following before continuing:

- ❑ Did you write the words of your thoughts, not just about them?
- ❑ Did you write at least a few dozen samples of inner monologue?
- ❑ Did you write samples of your inner monologue each day for several days?
- ❑ Did you write samples of your inner monologue from several parts of your life?

 Stop reading. Put the book down and do the exercise.

REFLECTION QUESTIONS

I recommend reflecting on your experience with this chapter's exercise before continuing. You can reflect about anything you found relevant, but here are some questions you may want to consider:

- ◆ Did you notice any trends in your inner monologue?
- ◆ Did you notice common thoughts?
- ◆ How do you think your thoughts compared to others'?
- ◆ **Where and how might you apply your experience in the rest of your life?**

Post-Exercise

I hope you found *Inner Monologue* effective and that it showed you about how that part of your mind works as much as it did with me. If you didn't already, look for trends in your inner monologue. Did you find yourself judgmental? Accepting? Negative? Positive? Thoughtful? Repetitive?

Personally, this exercise raised my awareness of how this part of my mind worked more than anything had before. I've meditated a fair amount. As much as I value the practice, I find *Three Raisins* and *Inner Monologue*, in maybe two hours of cumulative effort, teach as much that is useful for leading yourself and others as months of meditation. I've also done yoga for years. As accepted as meditation and yoga have become, almost nobody says, "Hey, Jim, let's get together Saturday and meditate for an hour," even in cultures that practice them more. I recommend meditation, but I recommend these two exercises first.

As for my results, I was surprised at the negativity and judgment, which I first considered a problem. Then I learned that everyone finds similar results, which told me *I'm* not negative and judgmental. *Everyone* is. The mind works that way. That realization liberated me from feeling guilty over my thoughts. It lowered my inhibitions to raise my self-awareness.

Knowing how my inner monologue works enables me to influence it, which influences how I see the world, how I react and behave, and how the world responds to me. It also helps me manage how I react emotionally, which increases my resilience, motivation, and other elements of personal leadership. The more I understand that others' minds work similarly, the more I can understand and lead them, too. It also increases my empathy and compassion.

We will build on this exercise for the rest of the exercises in this book. If you didn't get the chance to practice it as much as you liked, I recommend that you keep practicing as we continue.

CHAPTER 4

Write Your Beliefs

Peter Drucker told the parable of the three stonecutters in his 1954 book *The Practice of Management*:

> Many years ago, a passerby saw three workers cutting stones in a quarry. Though they were doing similar work, one looked unhappy, another looked content, and the third looked overjoyed. The passerby asked them what they were doing.
>
> The unhappy stonecutter replied, "I'm doing what it takes to make a living."
>
> The content one answered, "I am a stonemason practicing my craft."
>
> The overjoyed one looked up with a visionary glance and said, "I am building the greatest cathedral in the land."

Drucker, who focused on management, called the third stonecutter "the true manager" for understanding the importance of the whole enterprise, not just one's part. Harvard University president Drew Faust interpreted the parable similarly, saying, "The third stonecutter reminds us that the individual is not enough, that we want to make a difference in and for the world—as it is today and as it will be in the future."

I believe that they undervalued the parable, at least for aspiring leaders, in its ability to show that you can become a cathedral builder. The cathedral builder is the happiest of the three, is probably the most productive, and probably finds the most meaning in the work. The difference between their viewpoints is not innate or superhuman. Anyone could believe what the cathedral builder does, including the other two. They differ in what each chooses to believe.*

What I Mean by *Belief* in This Exercise

Our environments have more information than our brains can store or process. To make sense of everything we perceive, our minds filter out most of the information our senses give us and keep only what they think helps. Consider how complex your environment is. Other people are as complex as we are, and we don't understand ourselves perfectly. And there are seven billion other people, plus everything else—dogs, cats, trees, planets, stars, and so on. Our brains didn't evolve to represent reality perfectly. They evolved to handle what affects us. They simplify reality for a purpose. That's what I mean by belief (or mental model): *a representation of reality for a purpose.* We'll learn a lot more about beliefs, so you don't have to get everything now.

A younger me would have said about the stonecutters, "Well, one belief is right and the rest are wrong," but each stonecutter's belief is in some sense right. They aren't logically exclusive, although we may happen to be conscious of one at a given time— that is, only one may be in our inner monologue. Likewise, many beliefs that are in some sense wrong help us lead, like when some-

---

*Many say "what *mental models* each chooses to hold." I use the word *belief* to mean the same thing, preferring the single word. If you prefer calling what I call beliefs *mental models*, feel free. People often associate belief with religion, but I use the term secularly.

one says, "The Constitution is a living, breathing document." The differences in beliefs weren't about right or wrong but effectiveness.

Let's look at how beliefs affect perception, behavior, and our environments.

If you grew up with a pet dog and I was once bitten by one, we might have different beliefs about the same dog. You might see a cuddly pet. I might see a scary threat. You might feel calm and approach it. I might feel fear and back away. Your behavior might lead the dog to play with you while mine might lead it to growl at me. We both might conclude opposite things about the dog yet each feel right, with evidence.

The dog example illustrates how beliefs influence perception, moods, meaning, and behavior and how we influence our environments, which influence us back. The next few exercises will show that we have more control over our beliefs than most of us expect. Choosing our beliefs enables us to become cathedral builders and more. Leading effectively often means working with beliefs more than with facts and logic. What you consider irrefutable facts often turn out to be beliefs.

A psychologist who studied intelligence once told me that flexibility with beliefs was a major part of intelligence, which surprised me. They seemed unrelated. She explained that if you could only solve a problem one way, you would be unable to solve problems when your first perspective didn't lead to a solution. The more ways you can look at problems, the more problems you can solve. So besides helping you lead, the next few exercises may increase your intelligence.

Our beliefs affect how we perceive and interact with our environments—a tremendous and useful leadership tool. Few learn to use it because most people confuse their *perception* of their environment with the *actual* environment, concluding that they can't change things that they can. Your beliefs about the dog are not the dog, and you can change them more easily than you can change the dog. Many people understand the difference in the abstract but have trouble changing beliefs or even considering alternatives. People's greatest resistance to grow and develop often stems from inflexibility in changing beliefs or considering alternatives.

I could talk about beliefs and the skills to use them all day, but you'll learn more, faster through experience.

Speaking of Peter Drucker, by the way, he also called Frances Hesselbein the best leader in the country. In his words, "Frances Hesselbein could manage any company in America."

The *Write Your Beliefs* Exercise

Beliefs Filter Your Perception

The exercise is to pay attention to your beliefs and write them down. I recommend doing it for about a week or until you've written a few dozen beliefs, drawing from several areas of your life.

Beliefs manifest in our inner monologue, so this chapter's exercise builds on the exercise in chapter 3. This exercise looks at what *Write Your Inner Monologue* did, but a level up—at the idea level instead of at the word level. It also prepares us for the next few exercises.

We generally don't notice how our minds work with beliefs. For example, we often model other people with a few adjectives despite them being as complex as we are: "John is a good guy. He gets the job done and has a great sense of humor." You wouldn't want to be so simplified, but even such gross simplifications work most of the time.

Because beliefs filter out information, they never perfectly represent what they model. In that sense, every belief is wrong. But they still help. Because different people filter out different information, we all develop different beliefs, meaning that we perceive and react to the world differently, leading the world to react differently to us. Your own beliefs change over time.

When we plan and decide, we do so based on beliefs, not the objects of the beliefs. If you believe that there is a lion right behind you, you'll feel fear, even if no lion is there. You won't feel fear if you don't believe one is there, even if one is. You act based on your beliefs about John, not based on John. Since everyone has different beliefs, everyone chooses and acts differently despite living in the same physical world.

Those who recognize how beliefs work and know how to use them have an advantage leading themselves and others compared to people who think or insist that everyone sees the world in one way.

Examples

Consider the following beliefs about school:

- ▸ School is a place for learning.
- ▸ School is my last chance to have fun before working for the rest of my life.
- ▸ School is something my parents make me do.
- ▸ School is a place to get a job.

People with different beliefs will act differently even at the same school in the same class. You might believe one of those beliefs at one time and another at another time.

You and a friend might go to a party together. If you believe "this party is for talking and meeting people," your friend believes "this party is for dancing," and the music is loud, you might feel miserable and your friend might enjoy it. People with fixed beliefs might see that they can't change the party and get stuck in their misery. If you change your belief, you might like the party more.

Later chapters will cover ways to change beliefs and become cathedral builders. For now we'll work on awareness and flexibility with them.

Beliefs and Leadership

Motivating others often involves their beliefs more than the world directly.

Not all beliefs leading to different behavior contradict each other. For example, one person may believe "corn syrup is unhealthy." Another may believe "life is for enjoying." The former may avoid some foods sweetened with corn syrup that the other enjoys. Although they do opposite things, their beliefs aren't opposite. Subtle differences like that can lead to misunderstandings that undermine teamwork if a leader assumes beliefs based on behavior alone. Subtle changes in beliefs can lead to big changes in motivation and behavior in yourself and others.

Note that to believe something means that you believe it is true and right. But since all beliefs are simplifications and leave out information, scrutinize any belief you hold, no matter how right you consider it, and you will find flaws in it. It's still a belief. Just because you believe something is right doesn't mean someone else's beliefs wouldn't work better for you, like the cathedral builder. If you believe one thing and someone else believes something different but you think you both believe the same thing, you'll misunderstand each other.

Trying to impose our beliefs on others with different beliefs feels to them like self-righteousness and will provoke argument and resistance more than teamwork. (If you disagree, your reaction illustrates my point.)

What to Do

This exercise is like *Inner Monologue*, which it builds on. Instead of writing thoughts at the word level, this exercise is to write higher-level beliefs. They manifest themselves in your inner monologue, which is why we did that exercise first.

1. Carry a pen and paper with you for a week. (You can use your phone, tablet, or computer if you prefer.)

2. When you notice a belief, write it down.

That's it. It takes a few minutes a day. At the end, you'll have a list of many of your beliefs. It may take a couple days to get the hang of it, like with *Inner Monologue*, but if you practice diligently, you'll get it.

To clarify, if the exercise was to write what you observed with your senses, you might write something like, "My boss walked into the room," but that's not the assignment. For this exercise, you would instead write, "My boss sucks," "My boss rocks," "I hate working for other people," "Bosses make you do things you don't want to," or whatever beliefs you thought then.

That range of possible beliefs implies a range of different worlds. It helps to know which your mind lives in.

Some beliefs you'll notice once during this exercise. Others you'll see daily. Some more. Some will annoy you. Others will calm you. The point is to write them without judgment—just with awareness.

When I first did this exercise, I expected in a week I'd write 5 or 10 beliefs. By the end of the week, I had written about 70 and was writing new ones faster than when I started. Some were obviously beliefs when I wrote them. Others I wrote as strategies or in my own idiosyncratic way, which I had to disentangle to find the underlying belief. I saw that beyond identifying beliefs, I was developing a skill. Some students have written far fewer and some far more.

There's no right number. The point is to develop the skill to identify them across a range of situations.

The Differences Between Beliefs, Behaviors, and Strategies

We all try to live as best we can based on our beliefs. Because different people believe different things based on their unique experiences, simplifications, and so on, we behave uniquely. This book calls these behavioral choices *strategies*. Everyone's mental *processes* are the same: Beliefs lead to strategies. Like a computer, different inputs lead to different outputs even for the same hardware and software.

For example, if you read that corn syrup was unhealthy, you might believe "corn syrup is unhealthy" and develop a strategy of avoiding it, thinking things like, "I should check ingredients to avoid corn syrup." The belief about corn syrup being unhealthy leads to a strategy of reading ingredients. If you believe "life is to be enjoyed," never reading that corn syrup was unhealthy, you might develop a strategy to eat what tastes good without bothering with ingredient lists.

We spend more time thinking about strategies than beliefs because we perform them more. We may think about a belief for a moment and then implement a strategy based on it for decades. I occasionally find myself acting on some random thing a teacher told me in elementary school that I believed and never reconsidered in decades.

People doing this exercise often inadvertently write strategies instead of beliefs. You can usually distinguish strategies from beliefs because they focus more on verbs, action, and the word "should." Beliefs focus more on statements. If you find yourself writing, "I should check the ingredients to avoid corn syrup," or some other strategy, take the step to find the belief or beliefs prompting it until you find something like "corn syrup is unhealthy." Sometimes that's easy but not always.

Awareness of beliefs is more subtle but often more useful than awareness of strategies. Changing a belief will cause your strategies to change. If you try to change a strategy but not the belief that led to it, you'll likely eventually revert your behavior and reinforce the belief motivating it, which is counterproductive.

For example, if you have a strategy to cook at home more and eat at restaurants less, you'll have a hard time following it if you believe you'll never learn to cook. Whereas if you believe that home-cooked food is healthiest and with practice more convenient, even without a strategy, you may start cooking at home more.

EXERCISE CHECKLIST

I recommend checking off the following before continuing:
- ❑ Did you write your beliefs, not strategies?
- ❑ Did you write at least a few dozen beliefs?
- ❑ Did you write beliefs down each day for several days?
- ❑ Did you write beliefs from several parts of your life?

 Stop reading. Put the book down and do the exercise.

REFLECTION QUESTIONS

I recommend reflecting on your experience with this chapter's exercise before continuing. You can reflect about anything you found relevant, but here are some questions you may want to consider:

♦ Did you notice any trends or patterns?
♦ Did you notice unexpected beliefs?
♦ Did you notice the difference between beliefs and strategies?
♦ How do beliefs work?
♦ How do beliefs affect your life?
♦ Where and how might you apply your experience in the rest of your life?

Post-Exercise

Many people find the exercise challenging until it clicks and they start seeing beliefs everywhere, especially if they didn't do *Inner Monologue* thoroughly. Beliefs can be hard to recognize at first. Some challenges people often have include the following:

They think that if something is a fact, then it can't be a belief. You may consider something a fact. You still believe it. I believe the sun rose this morning. Even if it did, I still believe it.

They suppress beliefs that make them feel bad. The point of the exercise is to identify and record your beliefs without evaluation or judgment. Later exercises will show the value of working on beliefs that you normally suppress. The more you can identify your beliefs, the more you can work on them.

They are embarrassed by their beliefs or consider them un-important. Everyone has beliefs that seem weird, embarrassing, or whatever. The more you identify them, the more you can improve them. Suppressing them lowers your self-awareness. You don't have to tell them to others if you don't want to.

They think that if something is wrong, it isn't a belief. People used to believe the world was flat. Many believed smoking was healthy. We consider those beliefs wrong now, but they were still beliefs.

They don't work at it enough. Identifying beliefs takes skill, which takes practice developing. At the beginning of the exercise, you may find identifying them hard. Practice makes it easier. With enough practice, you'll start seeing beliefs all the time.

They write strategies instead of beliefs. Strategies result from beliefs. We spend more time thinking about strategies, so most of us can access them more easily. If you write something like, "I have to do X," "I like to do Y," or "I should do Z," you're probably talking about strategies. A belief motivates that strategy. With practice, you can find beliefs from strategies easily, which is a common way to access them.

They avoid writing contradictory beliefs. We all have beliefs that contradict others we also have. At one moment we think we're an idiot. A minute later we think we're a genius. Beliefs can't describe everything perfectly all the time, so some contradict others. Our brains didn't evolve to be perfectly self-consistent. They evolved by helping our ancestors pass their genes to us.

CHAPTER 5

Write Others' Beliefs

I ran into a friend, Christine, in Central Park. She worked at a small consulting firm. We hadn't seen each other in a while, so we caught up. She told me how she looked forward to her next assignment—a two-person strategy project in Mexico City. She was studying Spanish and looked forward to immersing herself in the language. I was glad for her but didn't think much of it.

I saw her again a couple months later. "How was Mexico City?" I asked.

"It's weird," she said. "We haven't gone. The project keeps getting delayed. Things keep coming up." Again, I didn't think much of it and we moved on to other topics.

The next time we crossed paths, a few months later, I asked again about Mexico City.

"I finally found out what happened," she said. "It turned out my teammate's mother told her Mexico City was dangerous. When she told us, she explained that she felt awkward taking cues from her mother but couldn't dismiss her mother's anxieties, either. So instead of resolving it, she delayed us with things like passport problems and dentist appointments. I'm not even sure if she did it on purpose." Christine explained that when this issue came to light, they handled it and the trip happened.

I first saw Christine's teammate as the story's antagonist for what seemed to me irresponsible behavior. Not confronting the situation inconvenienced the client and could have lost the project.

While I don't endorse Christine's teammate's withholding information, I now see it as a detail. All teams have people whose beliefs conflict. If such conflicts are inevitable, then a leader who doesn't take responsibility for handling them has abdicated that responsibility.

Now I see the engagement manager as the problem character, even though Christine only mentioned him in passing. In consulting, the engagement manager leads the team that works with the client. Like the coach of a sports team, the engagement manager doesn't usually work on the deliverables. Without a coach, each teammate could have a different belief about what kind of game they'll play: an offensive game, defensive, fast scoring, winding down the clock, or whatever.

Leaders set beliefs and strategies because otherwise each teammate can have different ones, which will affect their behavior and motivations. If Michael Jordan expects to get the ball each time, he'll get annoyed at a teammate holding the ball to wind down the clock. If he knows the teammate believes he should wind down the clock, even if he wants the ball, Jordan won't get annoyed.

Jordan's job is to play basketball, not figure out his teammates' minds. A coach who takes on that responsibility enables the players to play to their potential. A common way to illustrate the point is to ask which team will get more done, this one:

$$\nearrow \leftarrow \downarrow \searrow \rightarrow \uparrow$$

or this one:

That happened with Christine's Mexico City trip. Everyone involved wanted to do the project. Christine saw the city as an opportunity. Her teammate saw it as a problem. Same city, different beliefs, therefore different perceptions leading to different emotions, leading to different motivations, leading to different beliefs, leading to different strategies, which conflicted. The engagement manager didn't uncover this difference.

You might ask: Is reading her mind the engagement manager's responsibility? How should he know Christine's colleague's thoughts? She hid her beliefs for months. Doesn't that excuse the engagement manager? Thinking that way may protect your job, but other teams will outperform yours. The point is to know that people choose based on beliefs and that their beliefs differ and then to lead based on that awareness.

Anyone on a team who recognizes this issue and fills the leadership vacuum will be seen as a leader, independent of title or position, at least in part. Christine seeing and exposing the problem might have enabled solving it and taken her a step closer to promotion to engagement manager. Same with you in your teams.

When you experience that everyone has unique beliefs, not just to know it abstractly, you expect everyone to act differently. You don't believe that people are "just different," which would allow you to blame them and maybe sleep better in the short term but disempowers you and limits your long-term growth. We know intellectually that everyone's beliefs differ. You need experience to feel the difference, which is why this book gives you exercises.

In fairness to the engagement manager, uncovering others' beliefs can be hard. People often protect them since revealing them makes us vulnerable. People obfuscate their beliefs to fit in, to please, to avoid conflict, and the like. Often they don't realize they're acting on beliefs, let alone suppressed ones. Christine's colleague wasn't necessarily lying. She might not have known her beliefs—one of the problems with low self-awareness.

You can never know another's beliefs like your own since you can't access their inner monologue, but you can improve your skill identifying them. You have to start by observing their behavior and communication. People behave consistently with their beliefs more than with what they say. The engagement manager sounded not sensitive enough to detect the signs nor experienced enough to act on them.

Let's get you to see more of others' beliefs than Christine's engagement manager.

The *Write Others' Beliefs* Exercise

Seeing How Beliefs Filter Others' Perception Builds Empathy

This chapter's exercise is like the exercise in chapter 4, which it builds on. Instead of writing your beliefs, this exercise has you write others' beliefs. It builds on the self-awareness of *Write Your Beliefs* by putting your focus outward, to others' beliefs. It also develops your sensitivity to how people's beliefs show in their behavior. It's our first empathy-developing exercise of several to come. It will also continue to develop your awareness of your beliefs.

Others' Beliefs and Leadership

People often lead and manage people through external incentives, like bonuses, promotions, and vacations for success and threats of loss of responsibility and demotions for failure.

While external incentives motivate, they do indirectly, through *internal* motivations, which motivate directly. Connecting with people's emotions motivates them directly. This exercise develops the skill to connect with other people's motivations through their beliefs.

This exercise is only about identifying and recording beliefs, not judging or disproving them, which hurts your ability to lead. We reason *from* beliefs, not *to* them. We often don't notice them because they feel like truths about the world. People with different beliefs believe different things are true. That's a problem for a command-and-control authoritarian manager who would prefer everyone to follow orders but an advantage for leaders who see how teams contributing diverse strengths can lead to outcomes beyond what they could envision alone.

The best way to see others' beliefs is through practice. Most of you will struggle at first. It's easy to read my words and think, "That's useful to know. Next time someone has a different belief than mine, I'll notice it and avoid problems like Christine's," but you'll forget soon if you don't practice and revert.

After you do the exercise for about a week, you'll start sensing beliefs other people may not know they have. You'll start to discern beliefs from increasingly subtle cues. That is, you'll develop intuition, like a baseball batter who can hit a ball thrown faster than he can consciously react. People will think you were born with it.

Later exercises will use this awareness to inspire people. For now, we're still focusing on awareness.

What to Do

1. Carry something to write with for a week.
2. When something leads you to notice another person's belief, write it down.
3. When something leads you to notice a belief of mainstream society, write it down.

You can't directly access others' thoughts, so you have to deduce them from their behavior and communication. You can't verify your conclusions, either, but you'll likely find your skill improving.

At the end, you'll have two lists of beliefs—one of other individuals' beliefs and one of society's. It may take a couple days to get the hang of it, like *Write Your Belief,* but you'll get it.

Examples

If your parent once said, "You should become an accountant. Then you'll never have to worry about a job," you might write, "My parent believes stability is the most important consideration in choosing a job or lifestyle."

If a TV commercial touted the safety features of a car over everything else, you might write, "That car company believes potential buyers care primarily about safety for that car model." You might also write, "Society takes for granted that having a car is normal."

What Not to Do

You'll find yourself judging others and their beliefs. You can't help it, but as in *Write Your Beliefs*, write the beliefs without judging, evaluating, agreeing, or disagreeing—only with awareness.

Also, ascribing people's behavior to their identity doesn't get to their beliefs. The exercise is not to write "John interrupted me because he's a jerk," which describes your belief, not his, and is the opposite of empathy. You would write something more like, "John believes what he says is more important than what I say."

More Difference Between Belief and Strategy

Since you can only observe others' behavior, you'll notice their strategies over their beliefs even more than in yourself. If you find yourself writing strategies, no problem. Most of us start that way.

Strategies are close to beliefs. Work backward from behavior and strategy to beliefs.

For example, if you notice your manager chastising someone for poor performance, you might at first write, "My boss likes to berate people to try to get them to perform better." That's a belief of yours about your manager. Asking, "What belief would make that behavior make sense?" usually helps reveal the belief. You might then write something like, "My boss believes that pointing out someone's flaws is an effective way to help them improve them" or "My boss believes that punishing people for their behavior stops people from doing it."

Beliefs offer different perspectives than behavior alone. Understanding beliefs creates more empathy than just observing behavior and helps you lead more effectively.

EXERCISE CHECKLIST

I recommend checking off the following before continuing:
- ❏ Did you write your best guess at the beliefs, not just describing or labeling them?
- ❏ Did you write at least a few dozen beliefs for individuals and society?
- ❏ Did you write beliefs down each day for several days?
- ❏ Did you make sure you converted any strategies you listed to their underlying beliefs—for example if they use "should"?

Stop reading. Put the book down and do the exercise.

REFLECTION QUESTIONS

I recommend reflecting on your experience with this chapter's exercise before continuing. You can reflect about anything you found relevant, but here are some questions you may want to consider:

- Did you notice any trends?
- How did identifying beliefs feel?
- Did you feel like you developed a skill?
- How accurate do you think you were?
- Did you feel differently about people when you thought of their beliefs?
- Does reading people's beliefs make you think differently about leadership?
- Where and how might you apply your experience in the rest of your life?

Post-Exercise

I've found people get several types of results from this exercise.

First, they improve their skills to recognize and identify others' beliefs in general.

Second, as they learn to identify others' beliefs, not just their behavior, they stop thinking things like, "John acts like a jerk because he's a jerk." Instead of believing that people are crazy or different when they do things they don't understand—the opposite of empathy and compassion—they find commonalities, to explain others' behavior so it makes sense.

Third, this exercise leads people to look to learn about others when they don't understand their behavior, often replacing judgment with curiosity.

Fourth, students often describe themselves as having more empathy for others after doing this exercise. The more they see someone's motivations based in belief rather than innate differences, the more they see others like themselves.

This exercise also led me through a series of transitions about society's beliefs. First, I noticed how large parts of society tried to influence me for their benefit, like advertisers, politicians, religions, and other big institutions, often at my expense: *Coca-Cola wants to profit off ruining my teeth and health!*

As I continued the exercise, I came to see each person acting on beliefs that made sense to them, making them seem more human and enabling me to connect with them. That is, people working at Coca-Cola feel like they're selling happiness or something like that. I may disagree with them, but understanding them at least decreases my stress from things I don't have resources to act on. I'm sure many people think that things I'm doing don't make sense. This set of realizations decreased a lot of frustration and misunderstanding.

Disliking something I can't change doesn't improve my life. Understanding it does.

Leading Yourself

Unit 2: Leading Yourself focuses on changing beliefs, changing habits, discovering and speaking your authentic voice, and personal development. In this unit you will start changing how you view the world and see how that change affects you. You'll develop habits in personal and professional development, communication, and attracting people to work with you.

CHAPTER 6

Unwanted Beliefs

Michael Feiner is among the top in the field. His book, *The Feiner Points of Leadership,* still holds a 4.9 out of 5- star rating on Amazon a decade after release. He was Chief People Officer worldwide at Pepsi-Cola, where he worked for 20 years. His course that I took at Columbia Business School ranked among the school's most in-demand classes and won him multiple teaching awards.

I took his course in the fall of 2005—one of my first experiences formally learning leadership. I loved what I learned and respected him greatly, at first and in the end, though things were shaky in the middle.

I approached him once after class to ask a question. His answer led him to refer to his book.

"Do you have it with you?" he asked.

"I don't," I said. "I'm using the library's copy. It's on reserve, so I can only use it in the library."

He looked at me confused. "Why are you using the library's copy?"

I explained that I'd gone to the bookstore to buy it but a salesman told me that the less expensive paperback would be out soon and suggested I wait for it, so I did, using the library copy in the meantime.

He boomed, *"You're too damn cheap to buy my book?!"*

I stood dumbstruck. I couldn't believe my ears: *He cursed at a student!* Loud enough for my classmates to hear. And what was wrong with using a library copy?

My mind told me to retaliate. I don't remember what I did in the moment, but I know that I felt too outraged and confused to form a response. I probably just left, but I was already planning to counterattack.

Soon after, I went to his department to talk with other professors I knew. I intended to use the school's authority to outrank him, but I was frustrated to find that, while his fellow teachers seemed to agree that cursing at a student was unprofessional, they didn't act. Meanwhile I had to see him twice a week for class. (I had to admit that the course was still teaching me a lot.)

I was studying leadership outside of his class, too, in particular beliefs (the books I read then called them *mental models*) and how they affect our perceptions, emotions, and behavior. I began to see beliefs as something you could deliberately change.

What I learned showed me a few things. First, I distinguished my behavior—retaliation—from my emotions—anger, frustration, confusion, self-righteousness, and outrage—which enabled me to understand each more clearly.

Second, despite my fantasies of winning a battle, I noticed that I didn't like feeling these emotions or the behavior they were motivating. Who likes being angry? I felt like I was experiencing the saying that anger is like drinking a poison and expecting the other person to die.

Third, I saw that the emotions arose from a conflict between my belief about how professors should behave and what happened. I felt self-righteous because I believed I was right, but that was just *my* belief. *He* didn't believe he was wrong. So what did he believe?

Looking at my beliefs revealed a problem in me. They were making me miserable without affecting him at all. How could what felt like a natural response make my life worse? Could I do something about it?

I wondered if another belief might lead me to interpret this behavior differently. I thought: Cursing is sometimes appropriate. Friends curse around each other. Maybe he was being familiar.

I decided to try an experiment: to deliberately and actively believe he was being familiar, not a jerk. I had never tried anything like it before. Until then, I thought beliefs were right or wrong. At the time deliberately choosing to believe something felt weird. I felt like internally I still knew he was a jerk, that this belief wouldn't stick, and my beliefs would eventually revert. I tried it anyway.

I didn't tell him about my experiment. Nothing about his behavior changed. But *I started to see him as friendly*. Behavior that once looked callous looked familiar, even friendly. The more I kept at it, the more friendly he seemed. His jokes in class seemed funnier. He seemed more approachable.

The world didn't change. I did, and it improved my life. I became more calm, less angry, and less reactive.

After the semester ended, I continued to meet with him in his office for advice and never again saw the hostility of my earlier encounter. I can't say he and I became *buddies*, but I came to trust him as an adviser. Years later, when I started teaching, I sought him out for advice and found his among the most useful I got. I cringe at my initial self-righteous beliefs and the relationship they would have kept me from. How many other relationships was I selling short or missing out on?

I included the direct quote of him cursing at me to illustrate how dramatically different beliefs can lead us to interpret the same things. What I once found offensive I have come to see as one of the more barrier-lowering overtures from any professor in my long academic career. I wish more professors and leaders had the courage not to hide behind formality.

Actually, I did see what could have happened, years later, after he left teaching to work for a financial firm. Over drinks, a friend and business school classmate, Brad, told me that he had applied to work at Michael's firm and that he had interviewed him.

"Feiner was totally inappropriate," Brad said. "He asked me if I took his course. I said no. He wanted to know why." Brad said he tried to explain diplomatically that the popular course was hard to get into, that there were other great courses, and that he had to take others. Brad said he felt like Feiner was using his authority to pry and make him feel bad for not taking his course.

I said, "You know, I got to know him after taking his class. Is it possible that what looked like pressing may have been him being familiar?"

"No way," Brad snapped. "Not possible." He started to look angry, so I didn't press. I was scheduled to meet Michael soon after, so I asked him if I could ask about the interaction if I kept him anonymous.

"Go ahead. I don't care what you say to that guy."

When I met with my former professor again, I said, "Without mentioning names, an old classmate interviewed with you. I want to ask you your perspective. But I'd like to give you my interpretation first to see if I understand you."

He said, "Sure."

I recounted the story. "My friend felt you acted inappropriately by asking why he didn't take your course," I said. "But I bet you weren't being inappropriate. I believe you were trying to be familiar, as opposed to being professional and polite but distant. What he saw as polarizing was you bypassing formalities."

"Exactly," he said, smiling warmly. "I was trying to give him the opportunity to talk person to person and not be a résumé." We talked about how teams don't perform highly when they are too formal with each other and can't develop trust and teamwork.

Brad and I saw similar behavior and believed he was a jerk, making us both feel miserable. Brad refused to consider alternative beliefs, stayed miserable, and didn't get a job. I changed my belief, which calmed me and got me a mentor.

I didn't see a different side of Michael. There was no other side of him. One belief filtered what I saw one way and created outrage and anger, as with Brad, and a different belief filtered it another way. No intellectual explanation could have revealed how much the change in belief changed my perception, despite my having faked it at first.

The *Write Your Unwanted Beliefs* Exercise

Beliefs You Don't Like Still Influence You

This exercise is to write beliefs that contribute to emotions you don't like. It applies the skills of *Write Your Beliefs* and *Write Others' Beliefs* to beliefs that are harder to grasp.

Emotions don't appear randomly. They result from your perception of your environment, among other things, which your beliefs influence. Some that you don't like feeling, like anger, suspicion, impatience, and disappointment, arise from inner conflict. Your emotional system makes you feel a way you don't like until you fix the situation. Detecting beliefs that cause emotions we don't like takes skill and practice because parts of our minds suppress them. I think of such beliefs as slippery. When you try to group them to understand them, the emotions they evoke overwhelm and distract you and they slip out of your focus.

What to Do

1. Carry something to write with for a week.

2. When you feel an emotion you don't like, find what belief or beliefs contributed to it and write it down.

At the end, you'll have a list of beliefs. You may have difficulty finding or accepting some. You may want to change them more than write them down. For now the goal is to record them without judgment or evaluation. It may take a couple of days to get the hang of it, but if you work diligently, you will.

Examples

Emotions that you don't like feeling include anger, resentment, frustration, anxiety, impatience, disappointment, rage, jealousy, envy, hatred, and depression. You may feel none or some of them while doing this exercise.

You may, for example, at some point during the exercise, feel frustrated and trace back the emotion to feeling that you deserved something you didn't get. If so, then you'd write something like, "I deserved the promotion that my coworker got."

You may feel bored and note that you're thinking, "Nothing matters anyway because I can't succeed, so why should I try hard?" If so, you'd then write something like, "Sometimes I believe my work won't amount to anything."

After a heated argument, you may write, "I believed I was right and the other person was wrong." By the time you write it, you may have changed your belief, so you may have to work to rewind to how you felt while arguing. You might also write, "Later I believed the other person wasn't as wrong as I thought while arguing."

Why Focus on Beliefs We Don't Like?

In the movie *Rocky II*, Rocky's trainer gave him an exercise to catch chickens. As a heavyweight boxer, Rocky valued size and strength. Chickens aren't big and strong, but fast, slippery, unpredictable, and hard to grasp, turned out to have value. The exercise developed him from lumbering, slow, aimless, and clumsy to nimble, fast, deliberate, and agile, although he took months to get there and felt vulnerable in the process. Handling unpleasant beliefs develops mental skills like Rocky's physical skills.

The goal of this exercise isn't to make you feel *more* unwanted emotions but to become more *aware* of them and the beliefs contributing to them and to develop skills to act on them.

Another challenge is that we don't usually feel like writing when we're feeling these emotions. We don't like to acknowledge feeling self-righteous, vulnerable, or whatever unwanted emotion. But those are reasons we benefit from this exercise, to raise our self-awareness. You will want to change beliefs that create emotions you don't like—in other words, to lead yourself. Later exercises will show you how. For now we're raising awareness. One step at a time.

Challenges

Some challenges in this exercise include the following:

▸ Not wanting to acknowledge emotions you don't like
▸ Wanting to blame others for emotions you don't like
▸ Suppressing how your beliefs contributed to emotions you didn't like
▸ Not wanting to write while you feel emotions you don't like and forgetting them
▸ Trying to change the emotions or beliefs and then not writing them down

- Feeling so gripped by the emotion that you don't think of writing about it
- Feeling beliefs are too embarrassing, trivial, immature, silly, and so on to write about
- Being discouraged by laziness or depression that you don't do anything

If these challenges affect you, I recommend mentally noting what happened and going back to the exercise. You don't have to tell anyone beliefs you're uncomfortable with, but at least write them down to raise your awareness and to give you tools for future exercises.

EXERCISE CHECKLIST

I recommend checking off the following before continuing:
- ❑ Did you write your beliefs, not strategies or emotions?
- ❑ Did you write at least a few dozen beliefs?
- ❑ Did you write beliefs down each day for several days?
- ❑ Did you write beliefs from several parts of your life?

 Stop reading. Put the book down and do the exercise.

REFLECTION QUESTIONS

I recommend reflecting on your experience with this chapter's exercise before continuing. You can reflect about anything you found relevant, but here are some questions you may want to consider:

♦ How did this exercise compare with writing your beliefs?

♦ Were you able to separate your beliefs from the emotions they evoked?

♦ Were you able to separate your beliefs from your identity?

♦ How did you feel while thinking about the beliefs and emotions?

♦ How did that feeling change over the course of the exercise, if it did?

♦ Did awareness of the belief make the emotions stronger? Weaker? Different?

♦ Where and how might you apply your experience in the rest of your life?

Post-Exercise

We're starting to move from awareness of sensations, thoughts, and feelings in general to awareness of specific mental activity useful to leading, particularly leading yourself.

Our minds tend to avoid awareness of emotions we don't like. They still motivate us. Whether we're aware of them or not. Lack of awareness means behaving reactively—the opposite of leading. Without the experience of an exercise like this to make us aware of thoughts and feelings we avoid, many of us spend more time reacting to them than understanding or actively working with them.

Writing beliefs that lead to emotions we don't like often surprises us. For example, you may have found yourself writing, "I'm right and the other person is wrong." Everyone has felt that way, but few outright say it. Not saying it, even to ourselves, lowers our ability to do anything about it.

Awareness of these emotions—even, or especially, when we don't like them—enables us to lead ourselves. Consider impatience, for example. If you feel impatient with someone and think, "This person is taking too long," that's *your* belief. *They* don't think they're taking too long, so acting on your belief and interrupting them won't motivate them to finish faster, no matter how right you think you are. *Their* beliefs affect them, not yours. Sometimes *you* take too long. Even if you don't acknowledge the belief, the feeling it evokes will motivate you. Without awareness, you'll behave reactively. The same happens with any other emotion we don't like.

I hope this exercise got you to see some beliefs you want to change and that you found your awareness enabled you to change them more easily. We'll return to how to change them.

Awareness clarifies how to act on emotions you don't like. Lack of awareness makes you a slave to them. We often regret acting without awareness. This exercise may have helped you experience that others often act thoughtlessly and reactively. You probably understand and forgive yourself for behavior you regret. Do you understand and forgive others as easily? Do you think doing so would improve your ability to influence them?

Of the emotions we didn't like, most of us probably tended to notice intense ones most, like anger or envy. As you continue practicing, you'll notice increasingly subtle emotions you don't like, such as anxiety. The point, again, isn't to feel more things you don't like but to enable you to act on more things you can change. The more you can manage emotions you don't like, the better you'll feel and the more you'll behave how you want, not reactively, controlled by your environment. Also, the more you'll be able to use the same skills to lead others.

Emotions and Meaning, Value, Importance, Purpose

We've worked on the connections between beliefs and emotions. Have you started to notice connections between your emotions and things like meaning, value, importance, and purpose (MVIP)?

This book focuses on the motivation part of emotions. They also have a feeling part. How they make us feel contributes to our sense of something's MVIP to us. Someone or something that we feel good about we usually think of as having positive MVIP. If it makes us feel bad, we think of it as having negative MVIP. If it generates no emotion, meaning it doesn't change our lives, we think of it as having no MVIP.

Understanding the connection between MVIP and emotions, and how much our beliefs influence our emotions, shows the value of awareness and skill in creating beliefs. As we move further into Unit 2, we'll see and experience the MVIP of influencing our beliefs.

This connection between emotions and MVIP points to emotional awareness as useful for creating more MVIP in our lives and the lives of people around us.

CHAPTER 7

Authentic Voice

On April 4, 1967, Martin Luther King Jr. spoke out against the Vietnam War in a speech called "Beyond Vietnam: A Time to Break Silence." Some historians have called it his most important. It's as eloquent and reasoned as anything King wrote and spoke. The text and audio are online, which I recommend reviewing. As an early prominent person to speak against the war so publicly, King knew he would ignite opposition and risk losing support.

He had privately opposed the U.S. involvement in Vietnam for some time but hadn't spoken publicly against it before because he had a productive relationship with President Johnson and his administration on civil rights. Johnson was escalating the war, and King didn't want to jeopardize their collaboration. So why did he speak against Vietnam then? One main reason was that someone led him to.

Ask Americans to list great leaders, and many will list Martin Luther King Jr. I think it's safe to say that anyone who led him qualifies as a leader. So, who led him?

By the year before "Beyond Vietnam," the boxer born Cassius Clay had transitioned from mere athleticism, as great an athlete as he was, to great influence. Where once his greatest claims to fame were his Olympic gold medal and wins in the ring, now his extem-

poraneous voice—funny, poetic, fierce, insightful, thought provoking, and more—garnered him as much attention as winning his
fights. "Float like a butterfly, sting like a bee. . . . Your hands can't
hit what your eyes can't see" remains in popular vocabulary today.
Who knows where he came up with his rhetoric? If he prepared it
ahead of time, his memory and delivery deserve acting awards. If
not, his improvisation seems unbelievable, except that he did say
all of those things.

He didn't start as eloquent as he became. If you've worked on
public performance, like taking improv classes or practicing with
Toastmasters, you know that disciplined and dedicated practice, especially with effective instruction, helps you improve. A large audience forces you to improve fast or to give up. As the heavyweight
champion, his audience was the world. Too talented in the ring for
the public to abandon him, his trial by fire led him to develop his
self-expression skills fast.

People often describe his speaking as "without a filter," but without a filter implies he'd make more mistakes as he developed, which
he didn't. His voice became more clear and covered increasingly
subtle issues. He made fewer mistakes. He developed skills through
practice. He communicated increasingly authentically in more
parts of his life. His voice developed to include converting religions
and changing his name to Muhammad Ali, stating, "I don't have to
be what you want me to be," even at the cost of a boxing association
stripping him of his title. People who develop their skill to communicate so authentically describe the change as liberating and free-
ing. Ali seemed to grow more free, even when facing controversy.
Speaking freely leads others to speak yet more freely. They (the others) also tend to respond more openly themselves. Inauthentic
speech leads us to raise our guards. We don't know what ulterior
motives they have. When people's speech reveals their thoughts,
we feel we understand them better so we trust them more. We want
to be like them.

By 1966, the year before "Beyond Vietnam," the government drafted Ali. By then he'd passed his trial by fire of expressing himself authentically publicly. In response to being drafted, he said,

I ain't got no quarrel with them Viet Cong. No Vietcong ever called me nigger.

He was one of the first public figures to denounce the Vietnam War publicly, in a way no one could miss—certainly not Martin Luther King Jr.

I find the eloquence of Ali's response amazing. I can't help but respond by asking, "Well, if they didn't, then who did?" seeing the answer before mentally finishing the question: the people sending him to risk his life to try to kill them. You might consider him self-serving except that his words rang true for millions of people. It's hard to think of a boxer who took punishment as he did as cowardly. He further backed up what he said with personal sacrifice. During the prime of his career, the government revoked his license to fight in the United States, revoked his passport to fight abroad, and convicted him of draft evasion. The Supreme Court unanimously overturned his conviction, implying his punishment was unjust.

I can only imagine he was able to say what he did by having considered his principles deeply and thoroughly first—more thoroughly because of how public his trial by fire was. Speaking authentically helps you think authentically. In other words, I believe his clarity of thought and speech came from experience.

The next year, King delivered "Beyond Vietnam." By then, King had great authority. He'd won a Nobel Peace Prize, led many marches, led many organizations, and more. He had become a statesman. What authority did Ali have? He boxed, but had no advanced degrees or high posts in big organizations. The mainstream distanced itself from him after his conversion.

Yet Ali, without authority, led King, with authority. King spoke of Ali's leadership in this area despite the risk of associating with an apparent outlaw who had abandoned his religion. That's the power of an authentic voice.

This chapter's exercise has you practice yours. You don't need a public trial by fire to practice. When I assign this exercise in class, I show students videos of Ali speaking extemporaneously publicly and ask if they think they could speak like him. Nearly all say no. When I ask again after the exercise, they say it would take practice, but they could see it. The exercise makes overcoming an apparently insurmountable obstacle a matter of practice.

The *Authentic Voice* Exercise

Remember what you wrote doing *Inner Monologue*? This exercise is to say those things—to voice your inner monologue—without planning or preparing. Just to voice it.

What to Do

At least two or three times a day for about a week, voice your inner monologue out loud.

I usually start by picking an object, commenting on how it connects to my life or something in it, paying attention to my inner monologue, and voicing it as it flows. For the first day or two you can practice alone, even speaking to a wall, but switch soon to practicing with others. The exercise is not to share prepared facts or monologues. It means speaking freely about unprepared topics. As you naturally switch between topics, people will follow and see you as unguarded and genuine.

You may worry about saying overly personal or embarrassing things. You won't. You have plenty of other thoughts.

It helps if you speak slower than usual, not trying to voice every thought, just the ones on your mind when you have something to say and don't have an agenda. For example, I often say, "I'm trying to think of something to say, but I can't think of anything. Except now I'm saying something," which leads me to start talking. Then I'm in the mode to continue.

This exercise sounds hard but gets easier and even fun. Many students describe having more genuine conversations than ever, with new acquaintances and old.

Practicing it gives you a powerful skill to understand yourself better, overcome anxiety, and create connections. It's also our first interactive exercise.

It starts hard. You have to talk while you identify your inner monologue and prepare to share it with others—a whole other challenge compared to a writing exercise. If you're too anxious to practice with someone else, I suggest starting alone to warm up, talking to a mirror or even just a wall. These exercises build on each other. Writing your inner monologue was hard at first, but now you can do it. The same will happen here.

Most people first worry that voicing thoughts they normally hide will make them sound crazy or that they'll say something they'll regret. They fear insulting their best friends or saying something offensive. You'll quickly find that you won't accidentally do that. On the contrary, you'll find yourself saying things everyone thinks. Others will see you as genuine and authentic for saying what they recognize themselves thinking but are too inhibited to say. It puts you in the moment. I find it easier in social situations than professional ones at first, but you can do it everywhere.

With practice it gets easy and feels natural. In fact, you'll find inhibiting your authentic voice starting to feel unnatural. You'll recognize many of your personal quirks as universally human.

You'll find you can talk at length, following your inner monologue as it moves around. Remember how your inner monologue never stopped when you tried writing it? Here that works to your advantage. People will find it engaging and intriguing. They'll wish they could talk like you.

People will see you as self-aware, open, and honest. Often funny, too. This perception is helpful for leading others.

People like to see that your mind operates like theirs. They see you as unguarded and let down their guard.

This student's reflection on this exercise illustrates how to do it and its effectiveness:

Spring break was a great opportunity to immerse my authentic voice around others and practice my inner monologue. My friends and I went on a road trip to Charleston - it's also imperative to know that I was the only girl on the entire trip. I was definitely self-conscious and embarrassed to just talk out loud my thoughts to college boys who love to poke fun at me already.

The first time I tried it was 2 AM on the way to Charleston when it was my shift to drive, I thought it was the perfect time to introduce, test, and practice my authentic voice, also especially when the guys I were with were half-asleep. It was funny because I was whispering my inner monologue partly because I didn't want to wake them up, but also because I had a large fear that they would judge what I would say. But honestly, my thoughts were mostly based on the road "I need to merge now.... Great this car just cut me off...etc".

Later throughout the trip, we went to the beach a couple of times and as we were walking around and exploring that's when I was most genuine and real with my friends. I've known these guys since 6th grade so I already have had deep moments with them, but what was different was I got to speak out my exact thoughts at the exact moment - not past thoughts and opinions.

This was when I was most vulnerable with my friends and it actually caused them to reveal some things that were on their mind too. It was a raw moment for us as friends as well as a self-actualization of my own authentic voice. It's intriguing to me how developing an authentic voice is what separates leaders from followers. By being proud of who you are and voicing your own opinion - that's what distinguishes the strength of a leader and being confident in the decisions you make. I didn't realize how something so small, like revealing how your mind operates, can truly change how people perceive you and interact with you.

Voicing Your Inner Monologue and Status

Insecure people often try to impress others. Confident people talk about what they consider important without needing others' validation. For example, people like to follow people with status, so they pay attention to what's on their minds. As a result, high-status people often just say what's on their minds in interviews.

People who speak openly without trying to impress appear confident and we see them as having status. This exercise helps you behave that way. When you do, others will treat you with status.

EXERCISE CHECKLIST

- ❏ Did you practice speaking with your authentic voice a few dozen times?
- ❏ Did you practice with different types of people?
- ❏ Did you practice over a few days, under different circumstances?

Stop reading. Put the book down and do the exercise.

REFLECTION QUESTIONS

I recommend reflecting on your experience with this chapter's exercise before continuing. You can reflect about anything you found relevant, but here are some questions you may want to consider:

♦ Did your voice change?
♦ Did it feel more authentic? If so, how?
♦ Did you fear saying anything you'd regret? Did you say anything you regret?
♦ How do you feel about speaking more openly?
♦ How did others respond?
♦ Do you want to do it more? Less? Differently?
♦ Where and how might you apply your experience in the rest of your life?

Post-Exercise

Students tell me that they spoke more authentically than they expected they could during this exercise and then found others responding with similar authenticity, even those who had to start by talking alone to a wall. In other words, they led others through their behavior and enjoyed it.

Most of us want to speak more openly but fear saying something offensive, accidentally insulting a friend, or such. We protect ourselves by saying what we think we're supposed to or follow what we think are social rules. Meanwhile, we look up to and often envy people who speak more openly and kick ourselves when we don't speak up—that is, when we don't assert ourselves. Many confuse being assertive with aggression and to avoid being aggressive end up also not asserting themselves.

We often say one thing while thinking, "I'd better be careful not to say something else," not consciously aware of what we're holding back. In short, we are inauthentic by unconscious choice. People see in you someone who wants to share but is inhibited. This exercise is designed to enable you to choose consciously, based on successful experience speaking authentically.

Others also sense that we're withholding information and emotion—because we are—which stunts social interaction, leads them to withhold back, lowers our credibility, and lowers our ability to lead.

The challenge in overcoming these problems is to learn to share more information and emotion by choice, which can be difficult after a lifetime of unconscious inhibition. The way around it is how we learn most expressive skills: practice and rehearsal. Practicing basics makes complex skills easy. You'll quickly find you can say things you didn't think you could, enjoy it, and keep building. You'll increase your ability to lead without authority, like Ali.

With experience, you'll increase your range, comfort, awareness of what you hold back, ability to assert, ability to engage others, handle the occasional gaffe, and more. I predict you'll also enjoy conversations more and attract others to talk and share with you.

CHAPTER 8

Adopt a New Belief

On a cold, rainy, windy, late-autumn New York evening, I found myself hurrying up Sixth Avenue to my friend's birthday party. Gusts blew the rain in all directions. I huddled under my umbrella, trying to keep as much of myself dry as I could. I was still getting cold and wet, especially my feet. I was miserable and tense.

A few minutes later I found myself striding confidently, relaxed, and open in the same cold, rain, and wind. I felt joyful. When I noticed the change, I laughed out loud.

What happened in between? Where did the joy and confidence come from?

I had been working on increasing my self-awareness for about a year by then and had reached a level where I could create and adopt new beliefs without thinking about it.

I later retraced my thoughts. When I had noticed the cold making me miserable, I thought, "I don't like being cold, but does it have to make me feel miserable? When I ski I get cold and still enjoy myself." When I noticed the rain making me miserable, I thought, "I don't like getting wet, but does it have to make me miserable? I get wet in the shower and it feels good." These two lines of unconscious thought led me to think, "Cold and wet aren't *bad*. I just don't like them," and they stopped making me miserable.

The same environment was making the same physical sensations, but different beliefs were filtering them—beliefs I had chosen to adopt. You can adopt new beliefs, too. When you do, you change how you perceive and react to the world.

When I arrived at the party, I was no less wet or cold than I would have been otherwise, but I felt great. Everyone else arrived miserable. I had to wait a few minutes while they warmed up and overcame their misery. Since they didn't change their beliefs, they had to wait for their environments to change, which was less under their control.

Don't think you can change your beliefs? Consider this situation. You wake up one morning to find you left the window open, so it's cold, and you overslept, so you don't have enough time to get to an important meeting. You jump out of bed. You figure skipping breakfast will save you 10 minutes. You need to save more. This meeting is important. Being late could be disastrous. A long shower isn't as important as this meeting so you tell yourself you'll take as short a shower as you can. You turn on the water and jump in. Two minutes, tops! You'll do what it takes to keep it short.

Then you feel the hot water. The cold goes away. It feels so good. You think to yourself, "I can relax for a few minutes. I don't have to take such a short shower."

In an instant, your belief about the importance of the meeting relative to the shower reverses. You remember all the other meetings you arrived a few minutes late to and realized they weren't that bad. Your beliefs and values change. They can do so in an instant.

You can explain it how you want, but the change remains. If your mind can do it, your mind can do it. The next time, you can do it deliberately.

A shower is a simple, short-term change, but we can change complex, long-term beliefs, too.

Three books that influenced me the most illustrate this skill by ordinary people confronted with challenging situations—*The*

Diving Bell and the Butterfly by Jean-Dominique Bauby, *Gimp* by
Mark Zupan, and *Man's Search for Meaning* by Viktor Frankl.

In *The Diving Bell and the Butterfly*, the author tells about his experience after a stroke paralyzed his body except his left eyelid. Before his stroke, he was a successful journalist with a family.

Near total paralysis sounds unbearable. Most of our beliefs
about how to live a good life wouldn't help in such a situation. He
changed his. He wrote the book by blinking to a transcriber, over 10
months, working four hours a day, about 200,000 blinks at about
two minutes per word. He wrote about his unique experience.

The book was published in 1997 to excellent reviews. It became
a number one bestseller, with sales reaching the millions, and then
was made into a movie nominated for four Oscars, winning awards
at Cannes and other festivals.

What were his beliefs? While he saw his body like a diving bell—
a heavy chamber to lower divers underwater—he saw his mind like
a butterfly. In his words,

> My diving bell becomes less oppressive, and my mind takes
> flight like a butterfly. There is so much to do. You can wander off
> in space or in time, set out for Tierra del Fuego or for King
> Midas's court.
>
> You can visit the woman you love, slide down beside her and
> stroke her still-sleeping face. You can build castles in Spain, steal
> the Golden Fleece, discover Atlantis, realize your childhood
> dreams and adult ambitions.

Different views than most of us would expect! You can imagine how
his views on life changed.

Gimp's author tells his experience after a drunk driver partially
paralyzed his arms and legs. Before the accident, he was a successful athlete. Now his beliefs on living a good life failed him. Yet he
later said that if he could go back, he would not change what hap-

pened. Why not? Because he lived a better life *after* the accident. He took time to transition, but he won a Paralympic gold medal; played a major role in an Oscar-nominated movie that won Sundance; met the U.S. president; spoke to children and troops across the country; appeared on the *Tonight Show*; performed on stage with his favorite band, Pearl Jam; rock climbed; and did many other things he would not have otherwise. In his words,

> Rather than fight an impossible battle, one that was beyond my ability to win, I chose instead to focus on the life that was within my grasp, and that life happened to be in a chair. You can say I was surrendering to my injury, but I chose to look at it another way. I was surrendering to my desire to live a happy, fulfilling life. I found I could now align my expectations with my abilities. Instead of concentrating on what I couldn't do, I tried to focus on how far I had come. When I first arrived in the hospital, I was almost fully paralyzed. Two years later, I could bench two hundred pounds. I could walk close to three-quarters of a mile with my crutches. I had sky-dived. I had crowd surfed. I had realized that most roadblocks existed only in my mind. But my physical limitations were different. They were real. By accepting them, I wasn't admitting defeat. In fact, I was doing the exact opposite. I was realizing I had done everything in my power to overcome them. And if I related all this back to my old ideas of winning and losing, I guess I was declaring myself a winner once and for all. It had just taken me some time to recognize what victory was going to look like for me.

Again, different views than most of us would expect—more happiness and fulfillment, not just from someone who became paralyzed but for anyone.

Man's Search for Meaning tells Victor Frankl's story of living under Nazis for three years in concentration camps, including

Auschwitz and Dachau. Before World War II, Frankl was a physician and therapist.

He wrote of his discoveries about beliefs,

> We who lived in concentration camps can remember the men who walked through the huts comforting others, giving away their last piece of bread. They may have been few in number, but they offer sufficient proof that everything can be taken from a man but one thing: the last of the human freedoms—to choose one's attitude in any given set of circumstances, to choose one's own way.
>
> When we are no longer able to change a situation—just think of an incurable disease such as inoperable cancer—we are challenged to change ourselves.

When he couldn't change his environment, he changed himself—in particular, his beliefs. The result? He inspired millions. His book remains a bestseller today, named one of the 10 most influential books of the twentieth century. More relevant to him, changing his beliefs led him to find more meaning in life, even in Auschwitz— not only to endure suffering, but in his words, amid torture he was able to find not just tolerance or comfort, but bliss:

> We stumbled on in the darkness, over big stones and through large puddles, along the one road leading from the camp. The accompanying guards kept shouting at us and driving us with the butts of their rifles. Anyone with very sore feet supported himself on his neighbor's arm. Hardly a word was spoken; the icy wind did not encourage talk. Hiding his mouth behind his upturned collar, the man marching next to me whispered suddenly: "If our wives could see us now! I do hope they are better off in their camps and don't know what is happening to us."
>
> . . . a thought transfixed me: for the first time in my life I saw

the truth as it is set into song by so many poets, proclaimed as
the final wisdom by so many thinkers. The truth—that love is
the ultimate and the highest goal to which man can aspire. Then
I grasped the meaning of the greatest secret that human poetry
and human thought and belief have to impart: The salvation of
man is through love and in love. I understood how a man who
has nothing left in this world still may know bliss, be it only for
a brief moment, in the contemplation of his beloved.

Bliss! He didn't just endure. He made his life about love, salvation,
and aspiration.

These stories' value is not that their authors were superhuman
but the opposite. They were regular humans with the same emotional systems you and I have. Anyone can become a cathedral
builder. When you look, you find countless examples of people
changing beliefs to create happiness, MVIP, emotional reward, and
more in situations more challenging than you or I face. Henry David
Thoreau, in "Civil Disobedience," considered himself more free in
prison when imprisoned unjustly. Martin Luther King Jr.'s "Letter
from a Birmingham Jail" echoed the belief. Susan B. Anthony believed she had the right to vote and could act on it. Nelson Mandela
believed he could make a difference, even imprisoned for life. Think
of Napoleon in exile, Michael Jordan after not making the varsity
team, Gandhi after being thrown from the train for his skin color,
Oprah Winfrey after her network failed publicly, Steve Jobs ousted
from Apple, and so on. Most of all, think of yourself in the face of
your adversity. You aren't reading this book because you believe
you can handle every challenge leadership may bring. You're reading it, in part, to change that belief.

What they can do, so can we. Through practice.

They inspire me not just to admire them but also to believe when
I feel miserable or even less than as good as I could imagine: "If anyone, anywhere, at any time overcame greater material challenges to

enjoying life than I am facing now but created more joy than I am, then I can too."

Since I've never considered my physical condition more challenging than paralysis or Nazis torturing me, they inspire me to change my beliefs as they did to get results like theirs.

The *Adopt a New Belief* Exercise

Becoming a Cathedral Builder

We did several exercises to raise awareness about beliefs in Unit 1, *Understanding Yourself.* This exercise acts on that awareness.

This exercise is to change a belief deliberately. We know from experience that our beliefs change. Now we'll do it intentionally. We aren't changing reality, just our internal representations.

Start with Your Emotions

Use your emotions to find beliefs to change. Emotions you don't like arise from conflict between what you want and what you observe. Emotions you like arise when your beliefs are in sync with your observations. Bauby, Zupan, and Frankl's message was that when you can't change the world, you can change your beliefs and create as much meaning in your life as you want. You work with your beliefs, but your emotions guide you.

Trying to adopt a belief that will make your life worse won't work. New beliefs rarely take root without considering the emotions they will create. For example, thinking, "I can go to the gym twice a week for a year," if it means sacrificing something you like more than the gym, like time with your children or some equivalent, fails for most people. It creates too much emotional conflict.

Instead of seeking a behavior, which takes willpower, seek an emotion, which motivates without willpower, like joy from exercising.

What to Do

The exercise is to adopt a new belief following these steps, which I'll elaborate on:

1. Find a belief that leads to emotions you don't like.
2. Think of emotions you would prefer in that context.
3. Think of a belief that would create an emotion you prefer.
4. Consciously and deliberately think the new belief.

The first three steps of the process are fast. They can take a few minutes. The fourth usually happens over several days. You don't have to dedicate time to it, though; you can do it in the background of your regular life.

For example,

1. I feel miserable from the long, cold winter and believe the weather is causing my misery.
2. I'd prefer to feel fun, like a child anticipating or playing in snow.
3. I'll believe that snow makes me feel like a child.
4. [*Then think the new belief.*]

I happened to do this belief during one long, cold New York winter and found that it worked.

STEP 1: Find a belief that leads to emotions you don't like.

In *Write Your Unwanted Beliefs,* you wrote beliefs that led to emotions you didn't like. You've probably noticed others since. Starting with one of them usually works, though you can find a new one.

STEP 2: Think of emotions you would prefer in that context.

I recommend thinking of how your relevant role models feel in such situations.

Say you feel nervous asserting yourself in meetings, believing "people will think poorly of me if I say something stupid." If you know people who don't feel nervous, how do they feel? Maybe confident, responsible, or something like that.

You may think of several candidate emotions. You can choose which to work on in the next step.

STEP 3: Think of a belief that would create one of the emotions you prefer.

Thinking of alternative candidate beliefs can feel weird at first. Frankl, Bauby, and Zupan had strong motivations to adopt new beliefs. Yours may not be as strong. Still, this step is a major part of becoming a cathedral builder.

The first time may take a while. If you want to feel confident, you might think of a belief like "High-ranking people say odd things and nobody has a problem with them," "Nobody has considered anything I've said so far too odd, so it probably won't happen," or something like that.

You can copy others' beliefs if you want. If you know a role model, you can ask that person what he or she thinks in similar situations for ideas. There is no prize for originality, only feeling emotions you prefer.

Make sure the new belief has two properties:

1. That it is plausible—that your mind won't reject it without giving it a chance.

2. That genuinely believing the new belief will improve your life.

Write the belief concisely. It may take editing. The more clearly you can think it, the easier the next step will be. For example, to feel better about asserting yourself, you might write, "People understand and support people who speak out more than people who stay silent."

I don't recommend choosing the opposite of your current belief. Notice in Mark Zupan's quote how he first struggled with beliefs that clashed with his world. Choosing beliefs that enable you to take responsibility to act on them usually works better. Effective beliefs usually both enable you and require you to take responsibility. When he realized he couldn't overcome his paralysis, the belief "I lost" didn't create emotions he wanted. Blindly choosing the opposite, "I won," wouldn't be plausible. "I will find a new definition of victory" met both properties and gave him something to act on.

Examples

Here are a few examples:

OLD	NEW
I can't lose weight.	If others have lost weight so can I.
Commuting wastes my time.	I can use my commuting time productively.
The weather is cold and miserable.	People in colder weather find ways to be happy.
I have nothing to do but watch TV.	I have plenty to do besides watching TV.

STEP 4: Consciously and deliberately think the new belief.

For this exercise, when you find yourself thinking the old belief, consciously put the words of the new belief into your inner monologue.

At first you'll feel like the new belief is wrong or fake. Remember that all beliefs are simplifications, so they all have flaws. Scrutinizing any belief will undermine it, even your old ones that don't feel wrong. You aren't trying to change anything external, just a mental representation. Frankl reached bliss.

Keep going past that "wrong" feeling if you feel it. Fake it until you make it.

Since you chose a belief that you expect to create feelings you prefer, the new belief will increasingly lead you to feel emotions you like. When you feel them, indulge in feeling the emotional reward that accompanies it. Emotional reward makes the new belief stick and motivates you to keep developing the skill. You are training yourself to believe something.

You will also sometimes feel the new belief is wrong. Accept that it may be, but then so is any other. If you feel emotionally punishing feelings, do the opposite of indulging in them. I recommend acknowledging them and moving on to other thoughts.

Believing a new belief takes time, but usually a week will do it. Try to pick beliefs that

▸ You think many times in a week.
▸ Don't generate overly intense emotions.
▸ You expect will improve your life.

The value of this exercise is the skills it develops. Once you develop them, you'll be able to change beliefs at any time. You'll also become more aware of beliefs where changing them will reduce unwanted emotions. You'll feel more emotions you like, which will lead to a lifestyle with more MVIP.

The more you can change beliefs, the more aware you'll become of emotions you don't like because you can do something about them, and then you'll act on them.

Like the journey of a thousand miles beginning with one step, this exercise gives you the rudiments of a basic skill you'll learn to apply faster and more comprehensively with practice. Each time you do it, your skills will grow. Eventually you'll change beliefs fast and easily, making yourself a cathedral builder. You'll also learn to influence others' beliefs—an important part of leading we'll return to.

If It Doesn't Take Root

If the new belief doesn't take root, try again with a different belief or emotional situation. Beliefs that are easier to take root are usually less related to intense emotions, less connected to other beliefs, and work on shorter time scales.

EXERCISE CHECKLIST

- ❏ Did you follow the steps above? The goal is not just to change one belief but to develop the skill to change beliefs in general.
- ❏ Did you work with a belief long enough for it to change?

 Stop reading. Put the book down and do the exercise.

REFLECTION QUESTIONS

I recommend reflecting on your experience with this chapter's exercise before continuing. You can reflect about anything you found relevant, but here are some questions you may want to consider:

♦ Did your initial candidate belief feel fake?
♦ Did that feeling change?
♦ Did you feel like you could change not just *a* belief but beliefs *in general*?
♦ Did you sense how your mind adopts beliefs and changes them?
♦ Where and how might you apply your experience in the rest of your life?

Post-Exercise

I hope you enjoyed, developed skills, and got insight from this exercise. The exercises are becoming more active. We'll keep building on them.

When I first did this exercise 10 years ago, it felt alien. My existing beliefs felt right. Trying to change them because I didn't like them felt wrong, like putting lipstick on a pig. Since then I've learned that believing doesn't make it right—all beliefs have flaws, so they can't be completely right—and that initial beliefs are often less likely to be helpful than ones I intentionally create after reflection.

The skills this exercise creates help me every day. Instead of getting stuck looking at problems one way, I have the mental flexibility to look for other solutions until I find one. Inflexibility in beliefs restricts your ability to solve problems, as I learned from the psychologist who studied intelligence.

CHAPTER 9

Adopt a Challenging Belief

What do you do when you have a boss or join a team you don't get along with? Since nearly everyone will have problems with some bosses, managers, teammates, and coworkers in their careers, if you leave every job every time you have a problem with one, you'll have a résumé a mile long filled with two-month jobs. Here's how I applied the skills from *Adopt a New Belief*.

As business school ended, a friend told me about a venture he was cofounding in educational consulting. The team was finding high demand from important clients, including helping create the prestigious King's Academy in Jordan, modeling itself after the elite Deerfield Academy in Massachusetts, which the King of Jordan graduated from. The team of about a dozen mostly came from Columbia's Teachers College and Business School. They had diverse, complementary skills relevant to market needs.

Despite the valuable clients and able team, the team wasn't gelling. They didn't have startup experience and I did, so they invited me to join. I saw what was keeping the team from gelling, as well as what was generating the valuable clients. The CEO, Tom, had what I would call a strong personality. Tom dressed impeccably—stylish yet academic. He quoted literature, philosophy, and popular culture. He impressed clients, which drew them in. His confidence told them his team would deliver. Hence the demand they saw.

Internally, however, his forcefulness pushed hard on his teammates. He demanded a lot of everyone but didn't support them. You wanted to deliver for him while wanting to leave at the same time. With everyone feeling similarly, you didn't know if the team would make it.

It didn't take me long to decide I didn't want the position. I've dealt with bosses I didn't like. Why put myself through it?

Before declining the invitation, I thought, "I just spent two years in school learning to handle challenging work situations. I should know how to handle these things. Why don't I join the team and try putting what I learned into practice? I'll go as long as I can, and if it becomes too much I can always leave. The next time I have a challenging boss, the stakes might be higher and I might not have the choice to leave, so I should take this as far as I can." Mentally, I made it into my professional testing ground for what I'd learned academically. I joined the team as chief operating officer.

There remained how to handle Tom. As able as I found him, as much as we shared the desire to deliver to clients, and as confidently as I decided to join the team, he still grated on me. I probably grated on him, too.

I noticed that preparing to meet him felt like preparing to go to the gym—anticipating challenge, which felt daunting, and growth, which felt encouraging. I had to steel my nerves, plan my actions, prepare how to handle problems, and so on. Instead of stressing muscles to develop them, I was stressing my mind to develop it.

Lifting heavier weights builds stronger muscles. As I developed my leadership practice through working with him, I adopted this belief:

Tom (or any challenging person) is a leadership equivalent of a heavy weight, and working with him is like lifting heavy weights at the gym.

Once the belief took root, I noticed that working sessions left me exhausted but not stressed. I felt the exhaustion of a job well done, not exasperation. My belief was adding meaning beyond my expectations, relaxing and calming me. I came to look forward to interacting with Tom the way I looked forward to going to a gym—a big difference from walking away from practicing what I had learned in school.

After about a year, the team coalesced and I moved on to other projects. I look back now with gratitude at my relationship with Tom.

After the project I found a pleasant surprise, following my Tom-as-heavy-mental-weight belief. Having mastered that level of business challenge, I decided to look for a heavier weight—that is, for a more difficult person.

The pleasant surprise was that I couldn't find one. That is, I still found difficult people, but all their difficulties were within my skill to handle. The world didn't change. It had as many difficult people as ever. I changed. I found my world no longer had difficult people in it. I couldn't find one then, and I haven't since. It's hard not to say I created a better world, but more accurately, I learned to perceive it differently, through the lens of a different belief.

Years later I decided to apply what I'd learned to a bigger challenge—my relationship with my father. We'd never been close, argued a lot, and hadn't had a meaningful conversation since high school. I only visited with my sisters for holidays. I felt decades of resentment that I believed we could only overcome by getting to the root of everything and resolving it—a Herculean task I believed neither of us wanted to do.

My success with Tom led me to try something simpler. I chose to adopt the belief that if I behaved like I'd want to behave in the type of relationship I wanted with my father, he would respond in kind and behave in a complementary way.

For the first time in decades, I chose to visit him in Philadelphia on a weekend with no holiday, without my sisters. We walked in the park near his place and caught up and then cooked dinner together. There were some frictions, but I didn't lose my calm. In other words, I behaved as I intended. He seemed to follow suit, and decades of resentment felt overcome. Changing a belief worked where decades of debate failed.

Before trying it, I would have called that belief crazy or too difficult to try. Instead, it taught me, through experience, to value flexibility in beliefs and develop skill in changing them.

The *Adopt a Challenging Belief* Exercise

To sense a counterproductive belief and deliberately change it is one of the most effective skills in leading yourself. This chapter's exercise is to repeat *Adopt a New Belief* in a more challenging situation. Experience has shown me how much more people learn the second time. We'll apply the skills you learn in leading yourself to leading others, so your effort here will reward you for the rest of the book and every time you lead.

What Makes a Belief More Challenging to Change?

A few things make a belief more challenging to change. The main ones are:

- ▶ It creates more intense emotions,
- ▶ Other beliefs depend on it,
- ▶ It takes longer to change.

If you do this exercise for one week, try to pick a belief that works on a time scale of about a week or less.

What to Do

Find a new emotion coming from a new belief to change, where the belief is more challenging to change than last time. Follow the same steps as last time with that greater challenge:

1. Find a belief that leads to emotions you don't like.
2. Think of emotions you would prefer in that context.
3. Think of a belief that would create one of the emotions you prefer.
4. Consciously and deliberately think the new belief.

EXERCISE CHECKLIST

❑ Did you follow the steps above? The goal is not just to change one belief but to develop the skill to change beliefs in general.
❑ Did you work with a belief long enough for it to change?

Stop reading. Put the book down and do the exercise.

REFLECTION QUESTIONS

I recommend reflecting on your experience with this chapter's exercise before continuing. You can reflect about anything you found relevant, but here are some questions you may want to consider:

- ◆ Did you feel more able than last time?
- ◆ Did the skills start taking root?
- ◆ What did it feel like?
- ◆ Where and how might you apply your experience in the rest of your life?

Post-Exercise

For me, learning and experiencing this ability to effectively change my world felt like finding a holy grail—to create new habits effortlessly.

I hope you enjoyed and got insight from this exercise and that it reinforced and developed your skills in adopting new beliefs from chapter 8.

I hope you also saw more of how beliefs take root. Many new beliefs feels fake at first. When they create an outcome you want, you feel emotional reward—the feeling that this outcome is right and you want it to happen more—which makes them feel true. Indulging in the feeling of emotional reward they create accelerates the process.

Practice enables you to change your beliefs deliberately. Change your beliefs and you'll feel like you changed your world because you changed your perception of it. Then your behavior will change to fit your new view. In other words, new beliefs lead to new strategies and behavior.

Other helpful side effects of this exercise include firmness in your beliefs but also openness to change them if others showed you a benefit to it. Most of all, you will have more confidence in acting on your beliefs.

I've experienced feelings of doubt, uncertainty, and fakeness, too. Since they always come on the way to personal growth, I've learned to appreciate and look forward to them, where I once feared them.

Following the steps above and starting with knowing your old emotions and the ones you prefer ensures you're moving in a direction that's right for you.

We'll build on these skills with beliefs in later exercises.

CHAPTER 10

No, But, However

This chapter's exercise is probably the simplest in the book to describe, especially compared to its effectiveness. Some find it insidiously difficult to do, but when it clicks, it becomes a helpful, supportive tool for your growth and effectiveness leading yourself and others.

The exercise is just this: Don't begin responses to others with the three words *no, but,* or *however.* People rarely start with *however,* so it's more like two words. I recommend doing it for at least a week.

No matter how much I point out the exercise is to avoid *starting* responses with the words, people misunderstand the exercise to be to stop using them completely. This misses the point of the exercise. It's about relationships and communication, not being positive. The point is to avoid negating people and to see what changes.

Marshall Goldsmith created this exercise. He tells about how he fines his clients for each infraction, which he donates to charity. He describes some of his clients as "richer than God," so the $100 he charges per infraction is negligible, but their competitiveness engages them. He gives them the instruction and they respond right away, "But I don't . . ."

He says back, "That one was free, but the next one will cost you."

"No, no, no. That's not what I meant," they say.

"Three hundred dollars," he says back.

Last I heard, he's given over $300,000 to charity from clients' transgressions in this exercise.

In the face of a man named the number one leadership thinker in the world, with multiple number one bestsellers, who has made this exercise a major part of his career and whose clients love him, they're more focused on telling him why they shouldn't change than learning from him.

The *No, But, However* Exercise

Behave like a leader and others will respond to you like one. They respond to what you do and say, not what you intend, when your behavior differs from your intent, however unintentional the difference.

Negating people tends to provoke defensiveness and skepticism, the opposite of openness to your leadership. We commonly, however unintentionally and unconsciously, respond to people starting with the words *no, but,* and *however.* For example,

"It's a nice day today."
"But it's supposed to get cold later."

or

"I'm in the mood for Chinese food for dinner."
"No, let's get Thai."

You may not think the words make that much difference or may not intend for them to, but you don't get to choose how other people hear you.

What to Do

This exercise is simple to describe but difficult to practice.

Avoid starting responses to people with the words *no, but,* or *however.*

Use the words whenever else you want, just not to begin a response. After the exercise you can go back to starting responses with them, although I recommend you stick with the practice.

That's all. For most people this exercise sounds simple at first but fast becomes challenging.

If at first you think the words don't make much difference, you will likely think differently after you catch yourself a few times. It's hard to catch yourself consistently, so it helps if you tell people you spend a lot of time with to help try to catch you. You can make a game of it.

I've seen many trends assigning this exercise to hundreds of students and clients. The biggest problem are the occasional students who do the exercise perfunctorily, like with 50 percent of their potential. They tend to be the people who begin responses with *no, but,* and *however* the most before the exercise. Ironically, they have the most to learn but squander the chance. These bulls-in-china-shops "kind of" notice their blundering, but not really. The extra attention it would force them to pay to others could revolutionize many of their relationships. The attention to detail builds integrity. For many, the exercise leads them to realize that they negate the people closest to them most, undermining their relationships with the people they care about most.

People's most common explanation for half-assing the exercise is, "I don't *mean* anything by it. I'm just saying the words by habit, but I'm really saying something different." People don't hear what you mean, though. They hear what you say.

Again, the simplicity of the exercise masks its effectiveness and depth in focusing on others and integrity in saying what you mean. The exercise is not about words or positivity but relationships.

What to Observe

While the instruction is to avoid beginning responses with the words, the challenge becomes to figure out what else to say. You end up listening and thinking differently.

Pay attention to

▸ How your thoughts change when listening to others
▸ What you say instead
▸ How often you slip up
▸ How other people respond differently, if you notice

You could respond to "It's a nice day today" with "I also heard it's supposed to get cold later," for example, which doesn't negate the other person.

EXERCISE CHECKLIST

❑ Did you avoid beginning responses with the words for at least a few days?
❑ Did you do your best to catch yourself each time?

 Stop reading. Put the book down and do the exercise.

REFLECTION QUESTIONS

I recommend reflecting on your experience with this chapter's exercise before continuing. You can reflect about anything you found relevant, but here are some questions you may want to consider:

♦ What fraction of your *no, but,* and *however* responses do you think you caught?

♦ Did you notice changes in others' reactions?

♦ How do you imagine the different responses feel?

♦ How else could you begin your responses?

♦ Do you think others noticed a difference?

♦ Where and how might you apply your experience in the rest of your life?

Post-Exercise

I hope you learned something from this exercise. Some people find it harder than others. Some make a game of it. I learned a lot from it. I'll share some of my observations for you to compare yours with.

My biggest revelation was realizing how much people negate each other—not just myself, but everyone. Some people start most of their responses with *no, but,* or *however,* some consistently with *no, no, no, no.* I found it incredible how they unconsciously and unknowingly create hostility and counterproductive negativity. Seeing people like that inspired me to master this skill and avoid leading people to resent me so much. Marshall's wife told me he never transgresses. I haven't hit zero, but I'm getting close.

Next was seeing how much of a difference single words made, sometimes overriding the rest of what was said. People who agree with each other get into arguments because of words they don't know they're saying.

Those were more passive realizations. I also noticed active changes.

The main one was that I had to pay attention more to what people said. Starting your response with *no, but,* or *however* gives you a blank slate, erasing their meaning. Easy for you, but dismissive to them, which undermines your ability to lead and influence them. Not allowing myself to negate them forced me to listen to make sure to respond to what *they said*, not just to what *I thought* they said or wanted them to say.

I also noticed myself choosing what to say more deliberately.

Finally, and maybe most importantly, the exercise showed me how details matter. If you lead well except for a few annoying habits, you don't lead well. Attention to detail differentiates professionals from amateurs and artists from craftspeople. It builds integrity.

CHAPTER 11

Avoid Imposing Values

You've probably heard the personal development advice to think about what you want your gravestone to say. Or to imagine yourself at the end of your life and ask what advice you on your deathbed would tell yourself today. They're useful quick mental exercises. Rarely do you see them play out in person. I once did.

My mom remarried when I was seven. My two sisters and I acquired a stepbrother, stepsister, and stepfather. Thanksgiving and July 4 were spent at my stepfather's family's house—his two brothers; their families; and, hosting the all-American affairs; his mother and step-father. Squire, the friendly cocker spaniel, completed the Norman Rockwell scene.

Sam, the patriarch, was its center, along with his wife, Dot. At least six feet four and usually laughing, with warm eyes, a ruddy complexion, and a white beard, Sam looked like Santa Claus with a hint of Colonel Sanders. You couldn't ignore him in a room.

I was in graduate school in New York City when Sam died in his home outside Philadelphia. It happened that everyone in my immediate family was scattered around the world and couldn't attend the funeral, so I attended alone of our clan. Although I knew my extended stepfamily, I didn't know Sam's friends.

The funeral, although somber, was in a bright, sunny church. His family spoke respectfully and meaningfully, as you'd expect. At one point the pastor said, "If anyone else has anything to share about Sam, you're welcome to come up and say it," and stepped away from the podium.

I heard gasps a moment later, as a ripple of whispering in ears passed through the attendees. I turned to look to the aisle. A man about Sam's age had entered through the back door, from outside the group. I didn't recognize him. He wasn't famous, apparently just a family acquaintance. He was dressed conservatively, with nothing suggesting anything special about him. With all eyes on him, he walked in measured steps up the aisle to the podium.

"Sam was a great man," he began. "We disagreed on many issues. We fought. He was on the left and I was on the right." He described himself as a Reagan-Thatcherite, followed by issues he and Sam disagreed on.

His words led me to reflect on Sam's patriotism and notice a pattern I was too young to notice growing up. Sam's patriotism seemed to concern the working class and labor. I remembered, for example, Sam talk about when the Campbell's Soup factory left Camden, across the Delaware River from Philadelphia. Its last major source of working-class income gone, Camden's Mischief Night—the night before Halloween, when kids traditionally throw eggs and toilet paper in trees—gave way to vandalism and fires. He lamented the loss of America's middle class and its frustration and loss of confidence in Washington, D.C., making the nation vulnerable to "a man on a white horse" with a populist message to usurp power.

As the man spoke of their disagreements, I realized Sam's strong views never intruded on his friendliness and respect. That's what the man spoke of, too. He had his community of like-minded conservatives and found himself estranged from Sam's community *but not from Sam*. With Sam, he said, he could share his views, understand Sam's, and be understood by Sam, even when they disagreed.

He closed with the most honorable good-bye I've heard:

"We wish we had someone like Sam on our side."

History admires leaders able to work with and unify people who disagree. Abraham Lincoln's team of rivals from across the political spectrum and George Washington's unification of a young nation, still filled with Loyalists, top the list of such American leaders. Eisenhower balanced Churchill, Patton, de Gaulle, and more.

On a smaller scale, more recently, Phil Jackson coached feuding Kobe Bryant and Shaquille O'Neal to three championships in a row, after coaching Michael Jordan and Scottie Pippen to six, including three with the nearly uncoachable Dennis Rodman.

We similarly admire great friendships among people who disagreed with each other, such as Supreme Court justices Sandra Day O'Connor and Samuel Alito, who held diametrically opposed political views. Picasso and Matisse competed for stature in the art world but didn't hold back from praising each other, each allowing the other to influence him.

How do they do it? Many suggest that not judging helps, but after *Inner Monologue*, I don't think we can avoid judging, at least mentally. Having standards and values means we evaluate and judge. I value having standards and values. Leaders who unite clearly did. Only a leader with strong values could write the Emancipation Proclamation.

We often *want* judgment from others. That's why we watch judges awarding 9.8s and love seeing 10.0s in sports. So the problem isn't internal judging, or external.

I've concluded that the problem is when we *impose* our values on others. If people respect our values, they can disagree and we stay comfortable. If they go beyond respect, to support us for our values, we feel yet more comfortable with them. We wish we had them on our team.

Leadership at almost every level benefits from acknowledging other people's values, especially those you disagree with. In the

Academy Award–winning documentary *Fog of War*, former secretary of defense Robert McNamara described the strategy that worked during the Cuban Missile Crisis. The U.S. and Soviet leadership disagreed fundamentally on how to govern, who should lead the world, who was right, who was wrong, and more. The U.S. military leadership wanted to invade.

The U.S. civilian leadership, however, led by President John F. Kennedy, pursued a strategy of trying to understand the Soviet leadership and our military. Understanding the Soviets' interests instead of imposing ours on them—a military invasion being an extreme case of imposing on others—gave them a chance to withdraw without fighting. We've since learned that Moscow had authorized Cuba to launch the missiles, which Cuba had resolved to do had we invaded.

Not imposing calmed what imposing may have escalated to nuclear war. McNamara described their strategy:

> That's what I call empathy. We must try to put ourselves inside their skin and look at us through their eyes, just to understand the thoughts that lie behind their decisions and their actions.

You wish you have people like him on your side. This chapter's exercise is our next in developing the skill of empathy.

The *Avoid Imposing Values* Exercise

Support and Build Empathy

This exercise is similar to *No, But, However*, which it expands on. It's similar in having you avoid using words, but this time completely, not just beginning responses.

What to Do

Avoid using the words *good, bad, right,* and *wrong.* I recommend doing it for at least a week. If you feel enthusiastic, you can avoid other words that impose your values on others, too, such as *should, ought to, appropriate, balanced, better, worse, improve,* and *acceptable.*

I'm not suggesting avoiding the words forever, just for this exercise.

As with *No, But, However,* note if you listen, think, or talk differently. If so, what do you say instead? Also note if others respond differently, and if so, how. Note what you notice about values and judgment and how they affect your relationships, awareness, and communication.

I predict you'll use the words a lot less if you do this exercise diligently.

Tips

You can almost always substitute *like* and *don't like* for *good* and *bad,* rewording some sentences. Likewise with *agree* and *disagree* for *right* and *wrong.* For example, instead of "Obama is wrong on this issue," you might say, "I disagree with Obama on this issue." Instead of "That was a bad movie," "I didn't like that movie."

Compare "This is a good movie" with "I like this movie." If people disagree with you on the first statement, they either have to let your statement pass and imply they agree, which is uncomfortable for them, or speak up and voice their difference, which distracts from your message and may lead to an argument. You may enjoy talking about movies, but provoking disagreement in general, especially when you didn't want it, distracts from your ability to lead. It's harder for someone to disagree with the second statement, which describes your state of mind.

Statements that force others to accept your values, like "This is a good movie" provoke debate, often tangential to what we want to talk about. Statements like "I like this movie" tend to create dialogue and conversation.

Few people will notice if you use the second form instead of the first, but I predict you'll lead people into fewer arguments.

Also, like *No, But, However*, you can make a game of it.

EXERCISE CHECKLIST

- ☐ Did you avoid the words for at least a few days?
- ☐ Did you do your best to catch yourself each time? (It can be difficult.)

 Stop reading. Put the book down and do the exercise.

REFLECTION QUESTIONS

I recommend reflecting on your experience with this chapter's exercise before continuing. You can reflect about anything you found relevant, but here are some questions you may want to consider:

- ♦ What fraction of your value-imposing words do you think you caught?
- ♦ Did you notice changes in others' reactions?
- ♦ How do you imagine the different responses feel?

◆ How did you express yourself without those words?
◆ Do you think others noticed a difference?
◆ Where and how might you apply your experience in the rest of your life?

Post-Exercise

I made this exercise a permanent habit for myself.

I still catch myself using words that impose my values on others. I find doing so divisive, provoking resentment or disagreement when I didn't intend to talk about values at all.

Like *No, But, However,* once you get the hang of it, you start noticing others imposing values on each other. You see arguments that are irrelevant to people's conversation form not from disagreement but from word choice. You may also notice how much people confuse labels with meaning.

Most of all, I find it forces me to consider my values more, as well as others'. Its benefits are big and numerous, if you haven't seen them yet. It forces you to listen more, to speak more clearly, to respect others' values more, to think more before speaking, and more. I find I provoke fewer arguments. I find that avoiding imposing values forces me to communicate more precisely, especially about MVIP, which results in more MVIP in my life.

CHAPTER 12

Feedforward

Marshall Goldsmith created *Feedforward*, this chapter's exercise. It's name is a play on words with *feedback*. You'll see why when you practice it. It's quick, easy to learn, and simple (although not always easy), and, most importantly, it works. You can use it your whole life, learning from it each time you use it.

Marshall built his coaching practice on it over decades. As a testament to its ease of use, applicability, and effectiveness, his client Alan Mulally, as an executive at Boeing, used the technique enough that Marshall barely had to coach him. He soon became CEO of Ford and soon after that was named both CEO and Person of the Year.

You will master *Feedforward* as well. It only takes a few times practicing to get the basics. I still use it regularly, over a decade after learning it.

The *Feedforward* Exercise

The one person you can never see from another perspective is yourself, yet you wish you could the most. After all, everybody else sees you from another perspective.

Others' views are indispensable to improving your life and leadership skills. Most people get them through feedback. At work they get reviews from their managers. Athletes, actors, and other performers get feedback from coaches.

As much as feedback helps, it has limits, mainly that it evaluates the past.

Asking someone to evaluate creates communication issues. People often hold back what they think you won't like hearing or if you might react in a way they might not like. If you ask someone how you did on a project and they say, "You did part X great, part Y great, and part Z great," does that mean you did everything great or that they didn't want to tell you what you did poorly? You'll never know, not because he or she isn't a great friend, but because of inherent issues with communicating evaluation.

When you ask about the past, you're asking about something you can't change. To act on feedback, you have to translate information about the past into something you can do now.

Feedforward gets usable information and advice without the baggage of feedback. It looks forward instead of backward. It's a simple, two-minute practice that can get you more useful information than feedback. I'll give some background and then outline the practice in a simple script.

What to Do

Follow the *Feedforward* script 10 times for one behavior you want to improve.

Like you learn scales by playing *do re mi fa so la ti do*, not in other orders, you learn *Feedforward* by following the script. If you want to improvise, you can, but you'll do so more effectively after you master the basics. You'll get most of it after 5 or 10 tries.

The Script

1. **Identify** something behavior-related you want to improve.
2. **Identify** a person who can help and why he or she would be helpful.
3. **Say** to him or her, "I'd like to improve *[X]*. You've seen me [do X] and others who are great at it. I wonder if you could give me two or three pieces of advice that could help me improve at it."
4. **Write** the advice down. Clarify if necessary. Do not evaluate.
5. **Say,** "Thank you."
6. **Optional: Ask** for accountability.

For example, as a frequent public speaker, I might do it as follows:

1. I would identify public speaking as something to improve.
2. I'd identify people who saw me speak in public.
3. I'd say to each of them, one-on-one, in turn, "I'd like to improve my public speaking. You've seen me speak in public and others who are great at it. I wonder if you could give me two or three pieces of advice that could help me improve at it."
4. I'd record their answers, asking clarification if necessary.
5. I'd say, "Thank you."
6. Say that they recommended I tell more jokes. I might ask them to review a future presentation to make sure I included a few jokes.

You do steps 1 and 2 on your own. You can pick any behavior you want to improve—punctuality, sleeping better, interrupting less, losing weight, quitting smoking, saving money, and so on.

Tips

What you want to improve will determine whom to ask. If you want to improve something at work, you might ask colleagues or a mentor. If you want to lose weight, you might approach someone you know who lost weight. If you want to improve your relations with a family member, you might approach another family member or someone you know with great family relations. If you want to improve your first impressions, you could ask random strangers on the street.

The person you ask the advice from will feel like an expert, important, honored, and flattered.

Note that the wording of the exercise is precise. Marshall cut out many counterproductive things people say and included only what's necessary. *Feedforward* doesn't benefit from deviating from the script, at least not until you've mastered following it. For example, adding judgment, which beginners often do, will undermine it.

For example, people often say, "That's great advice," thinking it's encouraging. It still judges. How do you feel when you help someone and they judge your help? Even if they judge you positively this time, you know it may turn negative, so you feel motivated to avoid a next time.

Step 3 asks for advice, not evaluation or judgment. In *Feedforward*, you don't ask, "How did I do?" If you phrase your question to be about the past, people will evaluate your past, which creates the problems *Feedforward* is designed to avoid.

This exercise, done properly, gets the value of the feedback without its discomfort or limitations. If I ask people for *Feedforward* about public speaking and three people tell me I should use humor more, I can figure out that they don't think I'm funny, even though they would not likely have told me had I asked for feedback. Asking for feedback almost never gets you information like that.

Asking for clarification encourages them, as does taking notes.

In *Feedforward,* Quantity Creates Quality

Feedforward won't always result in advice you want or can use. When you get useless or unhelpful advice, still say "Thank you," since however unusable, the person still gave you advice. Then move on.

What do you do if you want to make sure you get advice you can use?

Do *Feedforward* with more people. Since it costs no money, takes little time, makes the other person feel good, and builds relationships, there's almost no downside to doing *Feedforward* with as many people as you like. Keeping track of all the advice you get lets you rank it. Act on the most valuable advice first and you'll generally improve before reaching the lower-value advice and never have to act on it.

Follow-Up

The accountability in step 6 can make the difference between only hearing advice and acting on it. Since most of us do what we're accountable to others, it will increase your likelihood of acting on advice and improve the quality of your work.

You have to think on the fly for how to ask them to hold you accountable. The advice and your relationship usually guide you. For example, if I asked for advice on public speaking and the person suggests speaking every chance I get, from making a toast at dinner to someone's birthday at work, I might say,

> Thank you, I would like to follow that advice. I figure I'll have a couple chances to speak per week. Would you mind if I check in once a week for a few weeks to make sure I'm following your ad-

vice? A phone call or email once a week is all I'm asking, though I'd welcome more advice on how I'm doing it.

Notice that I don't call the idea good or bad, which would evaluate it and discourage the person from helping.

EXERCISE CHECKLIST

- ❑ Did you choose one behavior to work on?
- ❑ Did you follow the script with at least 10 people?
- ❑ Did you avoid evaluating their advice?
- ❑ Did you say "Thank you" to each?

 Stop reading. Put the book down and do the exercise.

REFLECTION QUESTIONS

I recommend reflecting on your experience with this chapter's exercise before continuing. You can reflect about anything you found relevant, but here are some questions you may want to consider:

- ◆ Did you notice differences from feedback you might have gotten?
- ◆ Who is the leader in *Feedforward*?
- ◆ How did others seem to feel during *Feedforward*?
- ◆ How did you feel during *Feedforward*?
- ◆ Did you get any useless advice? Was that a problem?
- ◆ Where and how might you apply your experience in the rest of your life?

Post-Exercise

I use *Feedforward* often, as much or more now than when I learned it 10 years ago. It keeps showing me how much judgment in any direction (me judging others, others judging me, third parties judging others) hampers communication and provokes argument.

More importantly, *Feedforward* gives a simple way to bypass judgment while getting the value of others' perspectives. The more I use it, the more applications I see outside of asking for advice or as an alternative to feedback.

Noticing that *Feedforward* promotes productive conversation, I use it in social contexts like networking events, interviews, and such.

I also use it to resolve conflicts since it promotes communication but not blame or guilt. For example, when I find myself and another both trying to convince each other that we are right, I've learned to step back from promoting my agenda and ask the person for advice for his or her position. It usually lowers the intensity because they get to voice what they want without my assigning blame or admitting guilt.

I recommend trying *Feedforward* broadly, beyond "just" getting advice on your behavior.

Feedforward Interlude

Feedforward's applications are so diverse and effective that I consider it worthwhile to add an extra section for applications I've found for it that even Marshall hasn't written up.

Other Applications

Marshall presents *Feedforward* as a professional and personal development technique to improve behavior. If you use it for those purposes alone, you'll find it useful. It also gives value beyond "just" professional and personal development. As an argument it helped resolve on Sixth Avenue with an ex-girlfriend illustrates, conflict management ranks high among its applications.

Managing Conflict

On a bright, sunny spring day, she and I were walking in the West Village. We'd reached a stage in our relationship where we wanted to look good for the other, so she'd ask me what style of clothes I liked to see her in and vice versa.

Being a man and not a woman, I say things in a way that makes sense to me and don't hear things as she does. I say this because when I tell this story in workshops, the women often groan in dismay (maybe surprise?) at the wording I used to express myself. In particular, to tell her what I liked, when I saw a woman wearing something I liked, I would say, "She looks good in that."

While I thought I was answering her, evidently she had heard me compliment other women. This time she decided to give me a piece of her mind. A bright, sunny spring day in the West Village means lots of people, which complicates nuanced discussion. So commenced our talking past each other, her telling me how she didn't like me comparing her to other women and how bad I made her feel. My explanations didn't help. From your third-party perspective, you can probably see that we were trying to help each other.

At one point I had the presence of mind to realize that, independent of right, wrong, good, or bad, she wanted my behavior to change, which *Feedforward* does, without judgment or blame. So I used the technique.

I said, "It sounds like you'd like me to do something differently. If it would help us communicate, I'd like to try it, and it sounds like you have an idea of how I can do it effectively. I wonder if you could give me a couple pieces of advice for how I could do it."

She continued to tell me how wrong I was and how bad I was making her feel, apparently not noticing I had changed my message. It often happens in *Feedforward* that the other person responds with judgment even though you ask for advice, not judgment. They do what they're used to. Having practiced it many times in low-stakes situations, I was prepared for this higher-stakes, raised-voice, public situation. I remained calm and repeated the *Feedforward* script, politely but persistently. She still didn't catch on to my new message and continued telling me how wrong I was.

The third time, though, she caught on, thought a moment, and suggested how I could tell her my tastes so she'd understand.

I said "Thank you," told her I'd try, and then continued to ask her to hold me accountable by reminding me if I did it in a way she didn't like.

She said she would, resolving the months-long conflict.

While resolving one conflict may not sound like much, the technique applies more broadly. It has two main effects in conflicts: It's disarming and it lowers emotional intensity. It disarms other people's argumentative weapons by asking them for advice, not pushing or blaming. Lowering emotional intensity transforms arguments into problem-solving sessions.

(I can't help note that one of her pieces of advice was for me to tell her, "You would look better than her in that outfit," which contradicted her telling me that she didn't like being compared. She *did* like favorable comparisons, so it's not like she was communicating crystal clearly either.)

Networking and Interviewing

Another application arose from noticing something when I ran *Feedforward* workshops: No matter how much I told participants to spend no more than a few minutes with each person, they talked longer, often in deep conversations. I could barely pull them apart.

Instead of fighting the trend, I came to see that *Feedforward* is a simple, effective conversation tool, especially with new acquaintances, even for shy people. To understand its value in this context, have a friend do *Feedforward* with you so you feel it from the other's perspective. You'll feel what engages people: You feel like an expert, you feel flattered, and you want to hear how your advice works out, which leads you to want to see the other person again.

What more do you want in an interview than for the other person to want you back?

Although the exercise is about getting advice to improve yourself, you can ask for advice on anything. Listen for a person's interests, ask advice in that area, and you'll engage that person.

Getting Mentors

Teaching in universities, I see the time and money schools devote to finding people willing to mentor students. After finding them, the school has to act like a matchmaker, hoping the potential mentor's skills and experience overlap with some students' interests. Students often take the mentors for granted, like they were entitled to them for paying tuition.

Something is off for schools to work so hard to push something on students that they would value more if they worked for it. Mentor relationships give tremendous mutual benefit. If you want a mentor, you'll appreciate the relationship more if you find and create it than if someone hands it to you. Schools see the problem as a lack of mentors or access to them. I see it as students' lack of skill to create mentor relationships, which the schools' coddling exacerbates.

Feedforward gives you a tool to create mentor relationships, which will motivate you to find potential mentors and initiate.

Think of when you've given advice. You probably wanted to hear the results. You probably wanted the people you advised to succeed—after all, you felt you gave useful advice. If they had trouble, you'd probably want to help them more.

That pattern of wanting to participate in their success using your advice, will lead potential mentors to want to mentor you. Imagine that: Where universities work to give students something they don't appreciate and that mentors reluctantly relent to, you can lead valuable people to *want* to help you. Here's what you do:

1. **Identify and contact a potential mentor.** You have to figure out your criteria and how to initiate contact. The more you do this process, the more skilled you become.
2. **Do *Feedforward* with them.** You don't have to tell them you're doing an exercise. Ask for accountability, specifically requiring you to report back. They will nearly always

agree to this because you're showing determination and that you value their advice, which feels rewarding.

3. **Act on their advice.** It will take how long it takes.

4. **Report your results.** If they agreed to hold you account-able, they'll take your call or answer your email. It doesn't matter if the advice worked or not, just report your results.

5. **Do *Feedforward* again.** You don't have to tell them you're doing an exercise. They'll think you're asking more advice, which they'll appreciate because you're taking ini-tiative with them. Again, get accountability.

6. **Act on their new advice.**

7. **Report again on how it went.**

8. **You now have a mentor.**

After twice seeing you act on their advice and reporting back, they'll be happy to take future calls and emails. It's up to you to take the relationship in new directions beyond advice.

The more you practice *Feedforward*, the more applications you'll find. The key is doing it enough times to master it. Then you'll have a tool you can use the rest of your life. Your arguments will decrease in number, shorten, and turn into growth experiences, and you may get named CEO or Person of the Year.

Understanding Others

Unit 3: Understanding Others generalizes what you learned about yourself in units 1 and 2 to others. You will learn about the human emotional system—what leaders work with. In the process, you will learn how to act on emotions, including on your own, for more personal development.

Understanding emotions and their relation to MVIP is the main goal of *Unit 3, Understanding Others*. Partly you'll extrapolate what you learned about yourself in units 1 and 2 to others. Even if you understand and can lead yourself, you need to know about people in general and how to lead without using authority to lead others. "Leading" through authority breeds resentment and people wanting to undermine and leave, which is closer to the opposite of leading.

Think of the historical leaders you consider the worst people of all time—how many were authoritarian rulers? Meanwhile, what authority did Nelson Mandela have in his prison cell for 27 years on his way to becoming president? Or did Oprah Winfrey have over her show's viewers on her way to being named the "Queen of All Media"?

I'm not writing about emotions to talk about feelings gratuitously, nor do I suggest leaders should try to make others feel happy. Emotions are our motivations and are at the heart of MVIP. Like plumbers work with wrenches and pipes, leaders work with emotions and people. You have to master your understanding and skills with them in yourself and others to master leadership.

We have discussed emotions, self-awareness, leadership, and behavior a lot without clarifying what we mean by them. If we want to improve, it helps to know where we are.

CHAPTER 13

Write Your Models
for Leadership
and Emotions

When the company I cofounded nearly went bankrupt in 2003, the investors squeezed me out. It was emotionally painful and humbling, but I had a mortgage and needed to eat, so I couldn't dwell on it. I had to find a job.

Graduate school and starting a company hadn't taught me how to find one, so I did what I figured everyone did. I worked on my résumé and sent it everywhere. Luckily, a friend of a friend's company was hiring. They were in education and technology, areas I valued and had experience in. After a few interviews they offered me a job in product development, where I figured an inventor like me could enjoy himself and contribute to making the world a better place. I started enthusiastically.

Within months, I disliked working there. My work didn't challenge me. I felt stuck working on small projects that others created. I wanted meaningful work. I wanted to feel ownership. You probably know the feeling.

I suggested ideas to help the company, but no one acted on them. I tried moving to other groups in the company, but doing anything besides grunt work was hard. I couldn't figure out why. I finally gave up when they promoted someone hired after me to manage my team, including me. I felt snubbed and outraged that they didn't give me the job.

Still needing the money, I stayed but disengaged, not for lack of my wanting to engage but for no one there caring about me. I worked enough to earn my pay, but minimally. I did only what I had to, avoided responsibility and accountability, padded estimates of how long tasks would take, and so on. I looked for work elsewhere, caring about money more than what work I'd do. I felt defeated, but if working in a field I expected to like was disappointing, what difference did the field make? I might as well get paid more.

I also started to develop my ideas for myself instead of suggesting them to the company. A few seemed promising and didn't conflict with the company, so I began to develop them independently. Eventually I left to work on one.

Conscious that my lack of business training likely contributed to my first company's near bankruptcy, I applied and went to business school first. There, I learned a phrase that Michael Feiner created that summarized my frustration with my job more succinctly and effectively than any I'd heard: "People join good companies and leave bad managers." Nearly everyone I say this phrase to reacts with looks of "I learned *that* lesson the hard way" and "I wish I knew that earlier."

A lot of people tell me, as a coach, why they don't like their jobs. They complain about their managers more than their work, hours, or anything in the job description. Sadly, when I ask how long they've wanted to leave, many tell me "years." They want to change things but don't know how. They are looking for a solution outside the company for a problem inside it or themselves. They seem to feel like I did—helpless and resigned to believe that work means misery.

I believed that my choice of field would determine my job satisfaction and that my managers wanted or knew how to make me happy at work, or at least interested. I didn't understand what created satisfaction. I couldn't identify what made a job or manager good or bad.

Business school classes awakened me to what I was missing—relationships and emotions—but mainly in principle, not practically. My experience leading Tom, the CEO in *Adopt a Challenging Belief*, showed me I could lead people without relying on authority. Coaching developed it more, from seeing and helping others face the same challenges. I soon saw that you could lead more effectively *not* relying on authority, instead leading through emotions using empathy and compassion. So why don't people use emotions? Many only vaguely understand them, especially in business contexts. They see them as irrelevant to leadership.

I found the most effective way to start learning about emotions practically was to have people clarify what they knew. I came to see that people joined good companies and left bad managers because of fundamental misunderstandings about relationships; emotions; and what creates liking, disliking, emotions; and MVIP. Ignorance about emotions, motivations, and relationships led to incompetence using the basic emotional skills of empathy, compassion, and self-awareness.

The *Write Your Models for Leadership and Emotions* Exercise

We'll pause from the interactive exercises with an introspective one to clarify some concepts.

What to Do

Write two essays on the concepts below. I recommend writing them, not just thinking about the concepts, even if you plan to keep them confidential. Writing leads to deeper and more thorough thinking. It also tends to lead you to talk more about what you write about, attracting more leadership-minded people.

ESSAY 1: What Is Leadership?

We've approached only personal leadership so far—developing skills to lead yourself and avoid being reactive. Before we work on leading others, reflect on what leadership means to you now. Some questions you might consider include the following:

▸ What is leadership?
▸ How have my views on leadership changed over the exercises so far?
▸ What leadership experiences have I had so far?
▸ Who are my leadership role models?
▸ What do I consider success or failure in leadership? Good or bad?

ESSAY 2: What Are Motivation, Emotions, and Self-Awareness?

We've discussed emotions, motivations, and self-awareness without defining them. You've talked about them in this course and elsewhere. Since Plato and before and in many cultures, people have connected emotional awareness and skill with effective leadership.

Some questions you might consider and answer are the following:

▸ What is motivation?
▸ What are emotions?

- ▸ What is self-awareness?
- ▸ Why do they matter?
- ▸ How do they manifest in my life?

I recommend reviewing the questions a few times and letting the questions simmer in the back of your mind a day or two before writing your thoughts. After writing the essays, I recommend sleeping on them and editing them, even if you don't plan to show them to anyone else.

EXERCISE CHECKLIST

- ❏ Did you take enough time to think about the concepts before writing?
- ❏ Did you sleep on the essays after writing and edit them?

Post-Exercise

I have found the observation that people join good companies and leave bad managers to be insightful, with implications as broad as any other in leadership.

It shows the value of taking responsibility for your job (and career) and how you feel about it instead of depending on your managers for it. Several clients who desperately felt they needed to leave their companies no longer did after learning the perspective. Instead, they took responsibility and led their managers. Once they learned how to lead independently of authority, which we'll cover in Unit 4, they stopped feeling helpless. They started developing the skills to lead their managers to manage them how they wanted. They led themselves to create more MVIP in their work.

Next, it shows that your relationships with coworkers determine your day-to-day satisfaction more than your choice of field. It shows the incomparable importance, when interviewing for a job, of asking your interviewers about the culture and people you'll work with. Asking about the job description pales in comparison. Meet them in person. Ask why the person before left, what the rate of turnover is, and other questions about what working there will be like—*with the people you'll work with*, not just in general. Most people are afraid of asking questions like these, but they show interest and experience. Not asking shows desperation and neediness, among the most repellent qualities you can show.

Interviewers commonly ask, "Do you have any questions for us?" Most people respond by showing off how much they researched about the company or interviewer. They say things like, "I understand the firm recently acquired Company X. I wonder if you could describe how the post-merger integration is going," or something similarly impersonal or showing off. You could learn more, make a meaningful connection (which we'll cover in Unit 4), and show that you have more experience by asking about the people and management. How many jobs do you want to start blind to one of the main reasons people leave?

Next, when interviewing candidates to hire, you can learn about how they interact with others, not just validate their résumé, which will improve morale and reduce turnover.

Next, it tells you to focus more on relationships at work. Consider Toyota compared to the U.S. carmakers in the 1980s and 1990s. Toyota's cars were more reliable, more efficient, needed fewer recalls, and so on. The U.S. carmakers saw adversarial labor-management relations and perpetual costly labor disputes. Where did Toyota's advantages come from? Better technology? Technology doesn't come out of nowhere. People create it. Better people?

Toyota's managers and workers weren't smarter, stronger, or faster, nor did they have more hours in the day. Better systems? Systems don't come out of nowhere, either. Technology, productivity, and systems come from relationships between people and ultimately leadership.

Becoming more like Toyota and less like the U.S. carmakers in the 1980s and 1990s means learning more about people and our emotional systems and unlearning other things.

Next, it shows the importance of leading your managers. When you learn to lead people independent of authority or status (Unit 4), you can lead anyone. As it turns out, leading based on emotions is more effective than leading based on authority. It also creates MVIP and passion.

CHAPTER 14

The Model

I love the sport of ultimate frisbee, one of my great passions when I played competitively. For those who don't know, it's an intense, active sport, as athletic and exhausting as soccer or rugby. My freshman year, my college team made it to Nationals to finish fifth in the nation. As a freshman, I didn't contribute much, but the experience established my passion.

In college, we drove to tournaments in vans. After the last game each day, we would gather by the vans to change out of our cleats and sweaty uniforms, covered in dirt and often blood, exhausted, and hungry.

I would say, "Guys, we all want to shower, eat, and sleep. Instead of changing here, let's get in the vans and change on the way to the hotel. Then we can shower, eat, and sleep earlier."

No one ever followed. I couldn't understand why. My logic made sense. Why were they not convinced?

My teammate K.J., once explained, "Josh, what you're saying makes sense. But the way you say it makes me not want to do it."

I was somehow influencing people to do the opposite of my goal. Convincing didn't work.

Why was I trying to convince, anyway? If it didn't work, why did I keep at it? I think my tendency to lead through logic and convincing came from growing up learning to contrast reason with emotion. I learned that reason was systematic, and so concluded that emotions were unsystematic and irrational, even weird. They were for artists to express, not people to get things done with. Why bother trying to understand them, anyway? It seemed like trying to predict a coin toss. To conceive of empathy, compassion, and self-awareness as useful or well-defined skills I could learn was alien. Let artists deal with emotions, I figured.

Despite presenting emotions as irrational, my culture also enshrined the pursuit of happiness—an emotion—among its highest values, with life and liberty. In surveys, people ranked happiness as what they wanted most. In what they wanted for their kids, parents ranked happiness first.

With this confused and contradictory picture of emotions, no wonder I avoided thinking about them in favor of logic and convincing. In fact, learning more about emotions made them make less sense. For example, I learned that the root of the word *happiness* is *hap*—the same root of, perhaps, happenstance and haphazard—meaning "luck or chance." What does it mean for a culture's highest goal to be based on luck? Why pursue something that changes by chance?

My culture also told me that love, that other most valued emotion, came when struck by Cupid or Eros—outside agents. Fate and destiny are other outside forces, sometimes personified, predetermining our futures. We implore muses to inspire us, more outside agents (and the origin of the word *music*). *Inspiration* generally implies divinity, another outside force. *Enthusiasm*, from *theo*, meaning "god" (as in *theocracy*), means "with a god in you," again another independent agent. Cupid loved Psyche, another supernatural agent whose name, meaning "a supernatural soul," came to name the field of psychology. The word *disaster* comes from *aster*, meaning "star," as in *asteroid*, which means "bad star," implying astrological causes. *Star-crossed* means something similar, applying mainly to love, implying that the stars, not you, control your most important relationships. *Fortune* has the same root as *fortuitous—fort—*also meaning "chance."

I had little doubt that other languages and cultures had similar patterns, seeing as these lingual roots went back millennia and probably started earlier. I checked French, and its word for *happy, heureux,* comes from *heur,* meaning "luck."

With mainstream views of emotions favoring luck and supernatural agents over consistency, reliability, and predictability, no wonder I preferred logic, even when it didn't work. As a result, a decade after college, in business school, I was still trying to convince people like I did by the vans and still getting nowhere. This time it was classmates chatting at the start of study sessions instead of working. I would explain how we would enjoy talking more *after* finishing the work and how we might run out of time to finish our work chatting too long. My words had no effect. I told a leadership professor my frustration dating back to the vans. He laughed at K.J.'s explanation but didn't help me lead my classmates.

With logic and convincing getting me nowhere, I finally explored the value society placed on emotions. I would have to work with them, not just learn about them academically. I applied this book's exercises in beliefs and flexibility from units 1 and 2 to emotions to create a new model for them. Instead of trying to make one that was "perfect" or "right," I aimed to make one that was *useful.* Eventually, I came up with a model of the human emotional system, which this chapter's exercise covers, and a method for using it, which chapter 15 covers. This model enabled me to understand the human emotional system as consistent, reliable, and predictable— a foundation to build a leadership practice on. And a more rewarding life.

The point of presenting my model is not to tell you it's right, as you'll see, but to show you that you can create your own. Freud made his with the id, ego, and superego. Maslow created his with a hierarchy of needs. Cognitive behavioral therapy is based on one.

There are countless models for how humans work. Each has its uses. I've found mine useful in leadership, personal development, and professional development, as have many students. You can use it when it works for you. You can also change it and not use it when it doesn't work. Nearly every leadership tradition, school, and teacher has models for how people work. Few share theirs, forcing people to follow instead of becoming independent leaders. My goal is to enable you to be independent of them when you want or to draw on them when you want. To make you their peers

The Model Exercise

In chapter 13, you wrote your models for leadership, emotions, and self-awareness. In this one, you'll learn about a model for the human emotional system that I call *The Model*.

As leaders, we motivate people through their emotional systems like mechanics work on cars with wrenches and carpenters work on wood with saws. The better we know that system and the tools that work with it, the more effectively we can lead. *The Model* is a leadership equivalent of a schematic model for the internal combustion engine for car mechanics.

No model perfectly represents what it models. They simplify what they represent for a purpose. The purpose of *The Model* is to represent enough of the human emotional system to include the relevant parts for leading someone without being too complex.

First watch the three-part videos on *The Model* at *http:// spodekacademy.com/bookcourse-videos*, based on my in-person course.

Then do the exercise described at the end of the third video, which I describe below.

After watching the video, you should be familiar with *The Model* and its most important properties, which I'll summarize here.

The Model's Highlights

The Model represents the human emotional system and how it works. Again, it's not designed to be perfect or right, just useful.

Its main elements are environment, beliefs, emotions, behavior, and emotional reward. They operate in a cycle, as illustrated here:

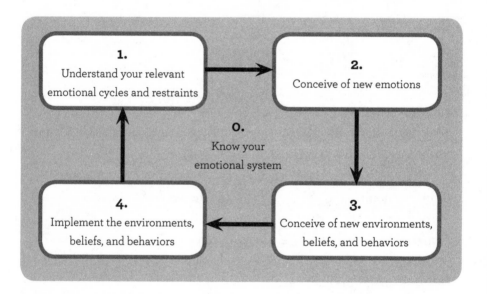

Emotions arise involuntarily based on your environment, beliefs, behavior, and the wiring we inherited from our ancestors to guide them to stay alive and reproducing.

You can't choose what emotions or emotional reward you feel, but you can choose how you act on them. You can also choose the rest of the elements—your environment, beliefs, and behavior.

Emotions are not good, bad, positive, or negative. They were evolutionarily useful for our ancestors.

The emotional system is consistent, reliable, and predictable, not random. Its outputs depend on one's environment, beliefs, and behaviors, so it may seem random if you don't know someone's environment, beliefs, and behaviors. Alternatively, the better you know someone's environment, beliefs, and behaviors, the better you can predict his or her emotions.

Your whole emotional system consists of many cycles, each interacting with each other—for example, ones for hunger, anger, satisfaction, and so on. Your mind has other parts than your emotional system, like your inner monologue, your executive functions, and so on.

Your emotional system evolved for our ancestors' environments. Where ours differs, its reactions may not be optimal for our modern world. For example, we often feel motivated to fight or run when stressed at work or to eat more sugar than is healthy.

Flexibility with beliefs helps you solve problems a fixed perspective can't.

What to Write

The exercise's written deliverable is write two situations you'd like to improve in your life in *The Model*'s terms. Start by writing the following:

Environment: _____

Belief: _____

Emotion: _____

Behavior: _____

Then fill out the details for your situation. For example, if I didn't like my situation at work with my manager, I might write,

Environment: At work, when I'm in person with my manager.

Belief: He doesn't listen to me or care about my professional development.

Emotion: Frustration and impatience.

Behavior: I do what I'm told, but I don't talk to him about what I don't like.

Or if I wanted to get more fit, I might write,

Environment: My apartment in the evenings, not working out, eating unhealthy food.

Belief: I'm never going to get fit so why bother.

Emotion: Resignation and complacency but also pleasure.

Behavior: Watching TV and eating unhealthy food.

Those are two examples of situations I dislike. I could also put an example I like but still want to improve.

Environment: In front of my computer once a day.

Belief: If I write in my blog every day, I'll create structure in my life and develop new ideas.

Emotion: Accomplishment and satisfaction.

Behavior: Writing my blog posts daily.

EXERCISE CHECKLIST

- ❏ Did you watch all three videos on *The Model*?
- ❏ Did you write at least two situations from your life in terms of its elements?

Stop reading. Put the book down and do the exercise.

REFLECTION QUESTIONS

I recommend reflecting on your experience with this chapter's exercise before continuing. You can reflect about anything you found relevant, but here are some questions you may want to consider:

+ How did *The Model* compare with your models for emotions and leadership?
+ What other models do you use for people, emotions, and motivations?
+ How would you change *The Model* for your use?
+ What happens when you break down situations in your life into environments, beliefs, emotions, and behavior?
+ What is the difference between pleasure, happiness, and emotional reward?
+ **Where and how might you apply *The Model* or your version of it in the rest of your life?**

Post-Exercise

I developed *The Model* to help me understand emotions and motivations to lead others and myself more effectively. Many historical figures had developed comparable models—Freud, Maslow, Jack

Welch (as I described in the videos), and so on—each designed for its purpose. *The Model*'s purpose is to understand the human emotional system in the context of leading others and yourself. No other model seemed to achieve the same purpose as well.

Since *The Model* covers emotions, happiness, and emotional reward, it overlaps a lot with the big questions of philosophy. I only took a few classes in philosophy, so I might be speaking in ignorance, but it seems to me that its biggest questions are what a good life is and how to improve yours—what Plato and Aristotle wrote about. If, as a twentieth-century philosopher said of European philosophy, "it consists of a series of footnotes to Plato," then everyone since has worked on details or less important questions.

I ended up studying Plato and Aristotle more after approaching leadership through Method Learning than in school. I came to see them as regular people trying to figure life out. When you don't see them as sources of quotes for term papers you'll be graded on, their writing becomes more accessible. Ideas like "the unexamined life is not worth living" and "know thyself" seem simpler, more meaningful, and more helpful.

Working with *The Model* has led me to see meaning, value, importance, and purpose as based in emotions. In Shakespeare's words, "There is nothing either good or bad, but thinking makes it so." That is, MVIP is not inherent to things but in our perception of them.

I've come to see something that creates emotions I like and emotional reward as having positive value, something that creates emotions I don't want or emotional punishment as having negative value, and things that don't create emotions at all as having no value.

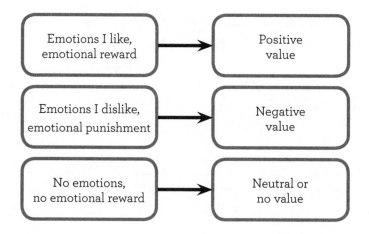

For example, there are millions of dogs in the world. A dog I spent years playing with and mutually caring for I value positively. A dog that growled at me and made me fear getting bitten I value negatively. A dog on the other side of the world that I'll never see or interact with I don't value much one way or the other.

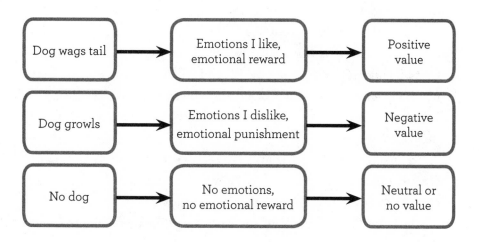

Value happens the same with people, books, and everything else. Meaning, importance, and purpose happen the same way as value.

Where emotions used to seem weird, ethereal, and ephemeral, *The Model* led me to see that I can sense them directly. Material things I observe indirectly, through my senses and in my memory, both of which are fallible. Realizing that I sense emotions directly has made them more important and accessible, which has filled my life with more MVIP. Since people create more rich, complex, intense, and long-term emotions than inanimate objects, and therefore MVIP, my relationships have also become more important parts of my life.

The result: Understand emotions and you understand MVIP, which means you know what a good life is. The concept of goodness is rooted in value, which is rooted in emotions. Since *The Model* bases emotions in evolution, implying that they are consistent, reliable, and predictable, it says that MVIP is consistent, reliable, and predictable, a major advance over believing that Cupid, the Muses, or the stars create them.

I had the advantage of knowing about evolution, which gave a billion more years of thyself to know. Even Darwin didn't know about twentieth-century discoveries like DNA, which helps us understand motivations like altruism.

The upshot for me is that *The Model* helps me understand MVIP, self-awareness, and the other important concepts to answer the first big question of philosophy. When I look at convincing, I think of what it motivates, which is debate. When you try to convince, as I did with my teammates and classmates, you inherently motivate people to debate.

In terms of *The Model*, a good life is one with as much emotional reward, emotions I want, and pleasure as I can create, of many characteristics, given my constraints of resources.

The rest of Unit 3 and Unit 4 answer the other big question: How do I make my life better?

CHAPTER 15

The Method

Nelson Mandela is widely regarded as one of history's great leaders—enough that if the Nobel Committee hadn't awarded him the Nobel Peace Prize, you would have said that they messed up, not him. Yet before winning the prize and becoming the father of a nation, he advocated violence. Many considered him a terrorist. What led to his development into a historic man of peace? What can we learn from that development?

Mandela was born in 1918 in a rural area of South Africa, where the white minority held political power. He was the first in his family to go to school. In 1941, he ran away to Johannesburg, where he became a lawyer and entered politics. He joined the African National Congress (ANC), a group promoting African unity and opposing European imperialism, and began moving up its ranks.

In 1948, the white-only South African government legislated apartheid—racist policies severely limiting the rights and freedom of nonwhites. The ANC and Mandela radicalized in response, joining with South Africa's Indian community to implement Mohandas Gandhi's nonviolent civil disobedience. The government responded with repression and violence. In response, Mandela, continuing to rise as an ANC leader, promoted violent action, although targeting only military and industrial targets, not civilian targets, which he considered terrorism.

After several times capturing and trying him, the government imprisoned him and his conspirators for life in 1964. He spent the next 27 years in prison, much of that time in an 8-foot by 7-foot cell with no plumbing, sleeping on the floor. The state did what it could to break him, including forced hard labor, repeated solitary confinement, and allowing him only one visitor and one letter every six months.

His accomplishments from prison would sound unbelievable except that they happened. As the nation's conflict grew increasingly polarized and violent, with global support on both sides (notably, Ronald Reagan and Margaret Thatcher supporting the apartheid government), Mandela emerged as a global leader. As one illustration of his influence, his seventieth birthday saw a tribute concert in London, watched by 200 million viewers worldwide supporting him. Despite mere reference to him being outlawed in South Africa, by the 1980s he negotiated *from prison* with South African presidents P. W. Botha and F. W. de Klerk.

Over the next several years he negotiated his unconditional release in 1990. He then soon met with Margaret Thatcher, Francois Mitterrand, George H. W. Bush, Bill Clinton, Queen Elizabeth, Pope John Paul II, Fidel Castro, and other global leaders across the political landscape. Internally, he navigated increased factionalism, conflict, polarization, and violence to lead negotiations leading to South Africa's first free election, mostly on the ANC's terms. People who met him overwhelmingly remarked that he acted without bitterness, vengefulness, or hatred. His Nobel Peace Prize came in 1993.

In May 1994, at the age of 75, with 63 percent of the vote, Nelson Mandela became South Africa's first black president in an inauguration televised to one billion people. To help reconcile the divided nation, he appointed former president de Klerk to Deputy President and instituted the Truth and Reconciliation Committee to expose and start moving past the nation's violent and racist past. In other words, he put the former apartheid leader—his former jailer—in a top position and granted amnesty to many who enforced it.

A prominent example of how he gained widespread support was by supporting the national rugby team that infamously symbolized apartheid power. Nonwhite South Africans despised the team and the international rugby community had protested and banned them since the 60s. With apartheid over, South Africa hosted the World Cup. In a highly visible and unexpected display, Mandela wore the team jersey to the final. On anyone else the jersey would have remained loathed by nonwhites and perhaps be seen as a token gesture to whites. Instead, when the team came from behind to beat its archrival, New Zealand, his actions helped make the victory for the nation instead of for the white elite.

These are the achievements of a historic master leader, qualitatively more effective and mature than before prison. Of course he developed in prison, but how? What resources did he have? What changed? How did he transition from angry, violent, confrontational, and polarizing to effective, peaceful, magnanimous, and gracious? How did he influence government leaders from prison? How did he learn to navigate and lead groups with conflicting interests, serving them while keeping himself at the forefront? How did he come to work productively with the groups he proposed bombing before without anger? How did he sustain support from allies worried he might sell them out?

What are you reading this book for if not to learn to lead groups to goals while keeping yourself at the forefront, even without institutional authority? If you've joined good companies and left bad managers, you've labored under managers who didn't appreciate you and discouraged you. Mandela's "managers" imprisoned him. He still led them and got their jobs. Still, he was human, like you. While his circumstances made his actions global, his leadership skills would apply anywhere, including in situations you face. If he could lead a president from prison, you can lead your manager.

Most histories recount the observable results of his transformation, but as leaders, our goal is to grow and develop ourselves, not just learn facts. Can we learn to grow like he did? Do we need 27 years in prison for it?

I believe Mandela explained his transformation best in several statements. Although stated at different times, I believe they combine with the Unit 3 exercises to show how anyone can grow as he did, without prison.

In his words, "Before I went to jail, I was active in politics as a member of South Africa's leading organization—and I was generally busy from 7 a.m. until midnight. I never had time to sit and think."

We all know the lure of working hard without first thinking, which takes patience and doesn't produce immediate results. Working long hours can make us feel productive without meaningful results. We don't distinguish between our *feelings* of accomplishment and *actual accomplishment* or between our *feelings* of effectiveness and *actual effectiveness*. Feeling accomplished and effective, however unjustified, reinforces our self-righteousness.

He also said, "I was a young man who attempted to make up for his ignorance with militancy."

The ignorance that led to his militancy wasn't of facts, history, the law, or anything external. It was of himself and how to understand and influence others. When he learned what worked, he used it, dropping the militancy in favor of understanding, empathy, and compassion, rooted in self-awareness.

These first two statements illustrate a common condition among people with more aspiration and conviction than experience: low self-awareness, leading to self-righteousness and ineffective action.

Then he began to learn the importance of knowing himself:

The first thing is to be honest with yourself. You can never have an impact on society if you have not changed yourself. . . .

Great peacemakers are all people of integrity, of honesty, but humility."

And how did he learn about himself? "Prison life, fortunately, I spent a lot of years, about 18 years with other prisoners, and, as I say, they enriched your soul.

How many of us would describe 27 years of imprisonment and forced hard labor as enriching our souls? Note the commonality in his experience in prison with those in the videos from chapter 14—Victor Frankl, Jean-Dominique Bauby, and Mark Zupan. They made up for physical constraints by increasing their mental freedom and flexibility.

Mandela, again: "I realized that they could take everything from me except my mind and my heart. They could not take those things. Those things I still had control over. And I decided not to give them away."

He sounds like Victor Frankl, suggesting a common pattern: "Everything can be taken from a man but one thing: the last of the human freedoms—to choose one's attitude in any given set of circumstances, to choose one's own way."

I believe Mandela is saying that his self-awareness came from knowing, in his words, his mind and heart—or, in my words, his emotional system. With everything else taken away and decades to reflect, he could learn them.

I believe this next statement illustrates his mastery of using his emotional system, not just knowing it:

The human body has an enormous capacity for adjusting to trying circumstances. I have found that one can bear the unbearable if one can keep one's spirit strong, even when one's body is being tested. Strong convictions are the secret of surviving deprivation. Your spirit can be full even when your stomach is empty.

Martin Luther King Jr., Gandhi, and Mandela spent time in prison and suffering. As King said in his "I Have A Dream" speech, "Unearned suffering is redemptive." They led others—tens of millions of people, including presidents and kings—from what seem like powerless positions from an authoritarian perspective. We want to be able to lead others independent of authority, through empathy, compassion, passion, understanding, and so on. Unit 4: *Leading Others* will show how. First, as these leaders say, you need self-awareness, humility, self-control, and so on.

Do you need prison to gain this self-awareness? Do you need to suffer?

I believe the answer is no.

Most leaders who use civil disobedience trace their practice to Henry David Thoreau—whom King, Gandhi, John F. Kennedy, Leo Tolstoy, Ernest Hemingway, and others named as an important influence. He wrote about it in his essay *Civil Disobedience*. During the Mexican-American War of 1846–48, which many considered unjust, he chose not to pay the poll tax, which he felt supported slavery and the war. He didn't oppose government in general, so he still paid taxes for roads, schools, and so on. The government jailed him in response.

You can see his transformation from one night:

> I have paid no poll tax for six years. I was put into a jail once on this account, for one night; and, as I stood considering the walls of solid stone, two or three feet thick, the door of wood and iron, a foot thick, and the iron grating which strained the light, I could not help being struck with the foolishness of that institution which treated me as if I were mere flesh and blood and bones, to be locked up. I wondered that it should have concluded at length that this was the best use it could put me to, and had never thought to avail itself of my services in some way. I saw

that, if there was a wall of stone between me and my townsmen, there was a still more difficult one to climb or break through before they could get to be as free as I was. I did nor for a moment feel confined, and the walls seemed a great waste of stone and mortar. I felt as if I alone of all my townsmen had paid my tax. They plainly did not know how to treat me. . . . In every threat and in every compliment there was a blunder; for they thought that my chief desire was to stand on the other side of that stone wall. I could not but smile to see how industriously they locked the door on my meditations, which followed them out again without let or hindrance, and they were really all that was dangerous. As they could not reach me, they had resolved to punish my body; just as boys, if they cannot come at some person against whom they have a spite, will abuse his dog. I saw that the State was half-witted . . . and that it did not know its friends from its foes, and I lost all my remaining respect for it, and pitied it.

Note his emotions: confidence in himself and pity for the state and his townsmen. You see the same pattern later leaders had: Their confining his body led to him creating mental freedom. He also wrote,

Under a government which imprisons unjustly, the true place for a just man is also a prison. The proper place today, the only place which Massachusetts has provided for her freer and less despondent spirits, is in her prisons . . . the only house in a slave State in which a free man can abide with honor.

In the words of *The Model*, he changed his beliefs about jail walls and where freedom lay, creating productive emotions he wanted, which created emotional reward. With that transformation, he didn't suffer. He seemed more amused.

These great leaders were as human as you and I. Their experiences didn't *create* new abilities. They *revealed* the human abilities they already had and that you have, too.

Mandela spent 27 years in prison. Thoreau spent one night.

I suggest that you need zero nights. I believe you need to develop yourself, which takes work, but not that you have to suffer. Learning *The Model* or creating your equivalent gives you self-awareness, and practicing *The Method*, which this chapter's exercise has you do, gives you the skill to change yourself without prison or suffering. I believe you need to master transforming yourself to transform others consistently and effectively. You need to act, not just know facts. Doing *The Method* enables that mastery. Your first time doing it may not transform you into the father of a nation. Your achievements depend on your outside circumstances, after all, but you will begin developing the skills, should the circumstances arise. You'll more likely start leading yourself, then your coworkers, your managers, people outside your organization, and so on. Still, there are plenty of national and global problems needing effective leadership to solve. No matter what challenges you want to take on, if they are meaningful, then creating MVIP for yourself and your teams will prepare you to address them. You will see the same mastery in nearly every effective leader. It's why the simple instruction "know thyself" has stood the test of time and why no leader calls self-awareness unimportant.

Your route to mastery, like Mandela's, is the same as for the musician who asked how to get to Carnegie Hall: "Practice, practice, practice."

The Method Exercise

What to Practice for Personal Mastery

In chapter 14, we passively considered the human emotional system. This time, we'll work with it actively. What better way to work with something than to use it to improve our lives? Since everyone's emotional system is similar, learning about the one we have most access to—our own—teaches about everyone's.

Our goal is awareness of and skills with both our emotional system and everyone else's.

What to Watch

First watch the following two-part videos on *The Method*, based on my in-person course:

http://spodekacademy.com/bookcourse-videos

Then do the exercise described at the end of the first video, which I describe below.

What to Do

The exercise is to do *The Method*, as described in depth in the videos and briefly illustrated here, in a situation that matters to you. I recommend doing it with a group of two to four people if you can, but it also works if you do it solo.

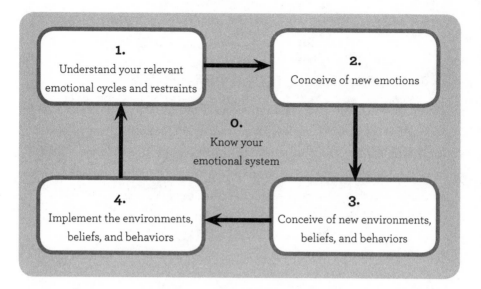

First, choose a situation in your life you'd like more emotional reward from. It can be the one from chapter 14 or a different one, ideally something you can change in the time you plan for this exercise (for most, about a week).

> **0. Know your emotional system**, which you learned about in chapter 14.
>
> **1. Write out that situation's environment, beliefs, emotions, and behaviors** (which you already did if you use one you wrote in *The Model* exercise) and **your constraints** that you won't or can't do in such situations.
>
> **2. Conceive of new emotions** you could have in such situations. I recommend thinking of how you think your role models would feel in similar situations or using your imagination.
>
> **3. Conceive of environments, beliefs, and behaviors** that will create the new emotions without triggering what you won't or can't do.
>
> **4. Implement the new environments, beliefs, and behaviors.**

When the environments, beliefs, and behaviors synchronize to create the emotion you want and you feel emotional reward, indulge in that feeling to help motivate you to do it again. When they don't, try to acknowledge it and move on to avoid discouraging yourself.

Example

I used to eat a lot of chips, pretzels, ice cream, and other foods that made me feel unsatisfied, guilty, and out of control. Some hurt my mouth because they were so sugary or salty. It took me years to change my diet to where I'm happy with it, eating a lot more fresh fruits and vegetables. The change could have happened a lot faster had I followed *The Method*.

If I could go back in time and choose my eating habits, in step 1, I would write the following:

Environment: My home, between meals.

Belief: The standard American diet is healthy. Preparing fresh produce is complicated.

Emotion: Craving, guilt.

Behavior: Snacking on pretzels, chips, ice cream, and such; buying products like them.

I would put some constraints on spending, not eating meat, preparation time, and complication to prepare food.

In step 2, I might take a cue from people who seem to enjoy food and feel satisfied from it:

New emotion: Satisfaction and joy

Then my target would have been emotions I like instead of what I used to imagine of fresh produce: confusion.

In step 3, I would have benefited from someone like me today suggesting the following:

Environment: My home, between meals.

Belief: The American diet is unhealthy. Preparing fresh produce is simple and delicious with experience.

Behavior: Snacking on fresh fruits, nuts, and vegetables; buy them and not packaged foods until I learn the basic skills of shopping for and preparing fresh produce.

In step 4, I would have done what I came up with in step 3. In fact, I did, but the transition took years. I love my current diet, but the transition could have taken weeks and given me years more of joy and satisfaction and less of craving and guilt, saving money and time in the process.

Changing a snacking habit isn't the biggest life change you can imagine, but the point of this chapter's exercise is to practice on something simple but meaningful. Some first applications that people choose include being more punctual, waking up earlier, interrupting others less, improving first impressions, exercising more, and things like that. Advanced applications include improving relationships with managers, improving relationships with parents, managing anger, and more complex, long-lasting changes, but I recommend developing experience and skill by practicing in simpler areas before advancing to them.

Many students tell me that breaking down situations through *The Model* into environments, beliefs, emotions, and behaviors enabled them to describe difficult challenges, sometimes for the first time, without creating emotional intensity that complicates the conversation. As a result, they find themselves able to act calmly and productively, with subtlety and nuance, on issues they felt anxiety, shame, or other discouraging emotion about before. Then they find themselves able to receive helpful advice, find solutions they feel confident about, and act on them.

When people ask you for advice, you may also find it helpful to apply *The Method* to help solve their problems. Breaking down their issues into their environments, beliefs, emotions, and behaviors may help them calmly and productively, with more subtlety and nuance and less anxiety, shame, or other discouraging emotion.

Doing the exercise takes effort. If you're not in jail or suffering, you have to impose the discipline yourself. You may feel awkward or even fake while doing it. Again, fake it 'til you make it. (That phrase is a strategy. Can you find its underlying belief?) You feel fake because you are changing something about yourself. By your old standards, the new you *is* fake. The point of *The Method* is to create a new you more consistent with your emotional system based on greater self-awareness. Some parts of you take time to catch up.

Beginning with self-awareness means sticking through that challenge, which will create more genuineness and authenticity for being more consistent with your emotions, by design.

Your first transformations may be hard, but experience will soon make later ones rewarding.

EXERCISE CHECKLIST

- ❑ Did you write out your situation and constraints (step 1) before acting on it?
- ❑ Did you start with your target emotions (step 2) to decide your new environments, beliefs, and behaviors?
- ❑ Did you indulge in feelings of emotional reward?
- ❑ Did you acknowledge unrewarding feelings and move on?

Stop reading. Put the book down and do the exercise.

REFLECTION QUESTIONS

I recommend reflecting on your experience with this chapter's exercise before continuing. You can reflect about anything you found relevant, but here are some questions you may want to consider:

- How does *The Method* compare with ways you have changed your life?
- What can you learn from Mandela, Thoreau, and their peers to lead?
- What heroes and role models of yours also went through personal growth?
- What is self-awareness to you?
- Where and how might you apply your experience in the rest of your life?

Post-Exercise

In its book, *HBR's 10 Must-Reads on Leadership*, Harvard Business Review included an article by Warren Bennis and Robert Thomas called "The Crucibles of Leadership." Bennis and Thomas interviewed many leaders and found that they shared a common type of experience. They wrote,

We came to call the experiences that shape leaders "crucibles," after the vessels medieval alchemists used in their attempts to turn base metals into gold. For the leaders we interviewed, the crucible experience was a trial and a test, a point of deep self-reflection that forced them to question who they were and what mattered to them. It required them to examine their values, question their assumptions, hone their judgment. And, invariably, they emerged from the crucible stronger and more sure of themselves and their purpose—changed in some fundamental way.

Do you *need* a crucible to lead? They imply you do, but offer no proof, only supporting examples. I suspect they didn't know any other way to develop deep self-reflection than externally imposed trials and tests. Just because many effective leaders experienced crucibles—even if *every* effective leader did—doesn't prove that you need one. You only need one counterexample to prove that you don't.

I recommend finding counterexamples that work for you. For me, a personal hero is Steve Martin, whom I consider a leader beyond "just" being a comedian, actor, writer, musician, playwright, producer, entrepreneur, and more. He led by becoming the first comedian to tour nationally to sold-out arenas. As Comedy Central's number six all-time greatest standup comic, he has influenced decades of performers—actors, musicians, writers, comedians, thought leaders, and more—not to mention his fans. Movies he directed, produced, and acted in have made the better part of a billion dollars. He won a Kennedy Center Honor, a Mark Twain Award, and an Honorary Academy Award.

His memoir, *Born Standing Up*, recounts someone who knew some things he liked and kept at them with discipline and diligence his whole life. He refined and developed his passions iteratively, but I don't think he endured a crucible. I don't mean to compare him with Nelson Mandela or others who went through crucibles. I only mean to show how one counterexample can change your model for what it takes to master leadership, or at least did with me. I would be overjoyed to achieve "only" at Steve Martin's level.

In any case, what constitutes a crucible depends on the person's beliefs. Someone born a Rockefeller might have so much material wealth and security that no one else would see them as having problems, let alone crucibles. But from their perspectives, they might still have to struggle. Siddhartha Gautama was born a prince yet went through struggles that led him to create his models and methods for personal development. His followers call him the Buddha and his practice Buddhism. Meanwhile, some people who live through what others consider great suffering consider their travails just regular parts of life. Use what works to help you develop and grow.

If you feel trapped and unappreciated at your workplace or in your relationships, you can consider your situation a crucible if seeing it that way helps, or not if it doesn't. Just because you aren't being physically tortured with hard labor or imprisoned doesn't mean your pain isn't as real to you as anyone else's is to them. The point isn't to compare suffering but to create a belief that helps you achieve your goals, in this case to help you become a leader.

CHAPTER 16

The Method, More Challenging

In *Adopt a New Belief,* I told a story about changing my belief walking to my friend's birthday party in the rain, transforming me from crouching down in misery to striding with confidence.

I left out a few details. That cold autumn evening was almost exactly a year after my "Home Run after Three Strikes" story from the first *The Method* video, which was my first time implementing *The Method.* In the intervening year, I had practiced doing *The Method* many times.

My unconscious thoughts—asking if the cold and rain should make me miserable, leading to my transformation—didn't *just happen.* They arose from practicing *The Method.* As I said I always do, I was walking down the street, gauging my level of reward, saw it was low, and asked myself how I could increase it through changing my environments, beliefs, and behaviors. My questions led me to think of times I felt joy being wet and cold, which told me my target emotion. In this case, I couldn't change the rain and cold of my environment, but I could change my beliefs, which I did, which led me to change my behavior to striding. Once my environment, beliefs, and behavior were in sync, my emotions followed and I felt confident. When the emotion took root, I felt reward.

This time was special because it was the first time I did it auto-matically, without thinking or trying. Using *The Method* effortlessly meant I had mastered the skill of turning misery into reward, like riding a bike. I felt tremendous exhilaration. I knew from handling my emotions in the cold rain that I would be able to handle discom-fort on the scale I felt them and likely more.

I'm not saying I expected perfect presence of mind every re-maining moment of my life, only that I recognized that I had devel-oped the basics of the skills of personal mastery and resilience that Frankl, Bauby, Zupan, Mandela, and these other great leaders had. Am I presumptuous to compare myself to people who experienced and achieved what these historical figures did? On the contrary. As best I can tell, the reason Frankl wrote his book was to help others—us—create meaning without having to suffer. Why else would he write,

> When we are no longer able to change a situation—just think of an incurable disease such as inoperable cancer—we are chal-lenged to change ourselves.

I believe he wants us not to suffer like he did.

The Method, More Challenging Exercise

Practice, Practice, Practice

Mastering *The Model* and *The Method* take experience, so this exer-cise repeats *The Method* with a more challenging application. That is, the exercise is to apply the same steps as those in chapter 15 to a situation that is more difficult to transform.

"More challenging" usually means choosing a situation that will

▸ Take longer to transform,
▸ Involve more intense emotions, or
▸ Affect more parts of your life.

Everyone's situations are unique, so only you know what situations challenge you more.

I recommend paying closer attention to the reward you feel when your environments, beliefs, emotions, and behaviors fall in sync. Does it come as soon as you start? Before you achieve your external goals? How does it feel? Can you accelerate or increase it?

When I teach in person, some students don't get *The Method* to click the first time. If you felt that chapter 15 didn't click, I recommend for you what I recommend for them, which is to apply *The Method* this time to an easier situation. That usually means one that is faster, less intense, and more self-contained. When it works I recommend to keep applying *The Method* to more challenging situations as you gain experience.

What to Do

Chapter 15 detailed *The Method*'s steps, so I'll only outline them here.

Choose a situation in your life you'd like more emotional reward from, ideally one you can change in the time you plan for this exercise (for most, about a week).

0. Know your emotional system.
1. Write out that situation's environment, beliefs, emotions, and behaviors and **your constraints.**

2. Conceive of new emotions you could have in such situations.

3. Conceive of environments, beliefs, and behaviors that will create the new emotions without triggering what you won't or can't do.

4. Implement the new environments, beliefs, and behaviors.

When you feel emotional reward, indulge in that feeling to help motivate you to do it again. When you don't, or you feel emotional punishment, try to acknowledge it and move on to avoid discouraging yourself.

Again, doing the exercise takes effort. You may feel fake until the new situation gives you reward. If you started with self-awareness, you will emerge more genuine and authentic than before you started.

EXERCISE CHECKLIST

- ❑ Did you write out your old environment, beliefs, emotions, and behaviors and constraints (step 1)?
- ❑ Did you start with your target emotions (step 2) to decide your new environments, beliefs, and behaviors (step 3)?
- ❑ Did you adopt and genuinely form new beliefs?
- ❑ Did you give enough time for emotional reward to kick in?
- ❑ Did you indulge in emotional reward when you felt it?
- ❑ If you felt unrewarding feelings, did you acknowledge them and move on?

Stop reading. Put the book down and do the exercise.

REFLECTION QUESTIONS

I recommend reflecting on your experience with this chapter's exercise before continuing. You can reflect about anything you found relevant, but here are some questions you may want to consider:

- How did applying *The Method* differ the second time?
- Did you have more confidence?
- Did you find yourself more flexible?
- How did changing yourself feel this time? Did you feel fake?
- Where and how might you apply your experience in the rest of your life?

Post-Exercise

In chapter 14, I wrote about how *The Model* helped me answer the first of two great life questions—what a good life is for me. A good life to me is one with as much emotional reward, emotions I want, and pleasure as I can create, of many characteristics, given my life's constraints.

The result is a life of meaning, value, importance, and purpose. I used to think of those terms as complicated and hard to define, but *The Model* simplified my understanding of emotions to see MVIP as describing emotional states.

The Method helps me answer the second great life question: How can I make my life better?

As I understand, Plato, Aristotle, and their peers tried to use logic and dialectic to learn or prove what a good life was and to improve theirs. Words, logic, and dialectic work for some things, but not all. They don't help you learn to play the piano or basketball, or to appreciate other people's performances. We know how to teach ASEEP performance. We do it through practice, not logic, and many great ASEEP performers become great leaders and live lives many of us want to emulate. Michael Phelps never took a course in philosophy, and would probably not trade his life for anyone's, not that you need to be an Olympic athlete to learn and master through experience life lessons that many philosophers can't imagine.

Consider the following progression of skills and realizations, which I designed the exercises in units 1 through 3 to create, among other results:

To recognize that we simplify the world into beliefs and know how beliefs work

To be able to choose a belief deliberately

To be able to choose beliefs *in general*—that is, to choose to believe what you want

To use *The Model* to understand your emotional system

That choosing beliefs (along with your environments and behaviors) creates emotions deliberately

That emotions create meaning, value, importance, and purpose

That anyone can create meaning, value, importance, and purpose deliberately, by choosing his or her environments, beliefs, and behaviors

This flow leads me to answer the second life question: How do I make my life better? The answer is to develop the skills of being aware of your emotional state and then choose your environments, beliefs, and behaviors to create the emotions you want, which is practicing *The Method*, based in *The Model*. Doing so will increase your self-awareness, which means knowing your emotional system and emotional state.

I'm not saying that *The Method* is the only way to create MVIP, but it works consistently, reliably, and predictably, and you can use it as much as you want. This book's leadership exercises turn out to be life exercises.

Putting it simply, you can answer life's great questions more effectively ASEEP-style than through logic and words. This book's progression leading to *The Model* and *The Method* are one such approach. Unit 4 builds on these results, so there is more to come.

As far as I know, this book's progression is the first Method Learning approach to leadership training, as Stanislavsky began in acting training. For me, at least, this approach applies beyond leadership to living life better, and more effectively than Plato and Aristotle's logic-based approach. I didn't study philosophy or its history, but if Western philosophy has been footnotes to Plato, then the traditional academic approach to addressing life's big questions has been missing this active approach. I value the education I got, but I can see that teaching *about* leadership but not *how* to lead, my education taught me at most about a good life, but not *how to live one*. When you think of people whose lives you want to emulate, do you think of university professors of philosophy or psychology? By their logic, they should know the most of how to live a good life—but do they live them?

Your Leadership Project

We're starting Unit 4, which begins leading other people. You can do its exercises with anyone, but you'll engage and learn more if you apply them to a project you care about with people you care about. You'll hear in the interviews with Chris how he did so, which led to big improvements to his life and ability to lead.

The *Your Leadership Project* Exercise

Before beginning Unit 4's exercises with others, this exercise is to create a *Personal Leadership Project*: something you want to do that matters to you and involves at least one other person to finish it.

The project should have some measures of success, failure, and accountability of your performance. You can change projects in the middle if necessary, as long as new projects meet the criteria below.

Past projects include

▶ Organizing a speaker panel on a subject you care about for an audience
▶ Proposing an idea to your manager for you to own and run
▶ Getting yourself promoted
▶ Creating an affinity group, like a book club, training workshop, etc
▶ Creating a new venture
▶ Organizing your community around a common interest

. . . and more.

With each exercise in Unit 4, I recommend practicing with friends, family, and others you know will support you, then to applying them to people in your project.

When you write your reflections for the rest of Unit 4's exercises, I recommend writing first about your experience practicing the exercises outside the project, then writing about your experiences practicing them with people in the project, when something you care about is on the line.

Unlike other exercises, where I suggest you take the time you feel right to do it, *I recommend writing your project within 24 hours*. If you are concerned about choosing the best project for yourself and you are having trouble choosing among more than one candidate, experience has shown that the best way to find the best project is to start one of them. If it turns out to be the best, you can continue confidently. If not, working on a project has led people to figure out which is best for them more effectively than thinking about projects without acting. In any case, the goal for this project is to start small so you can build on it.

What to Do

You won't start working on the project now, only writing about it.

Think of a project you'd like to do that you can't do alone and you think you could handle with a helper or two. Then, for the reflection, write the following:

The Problem: what is the situation now and what is your goal?

I recommend choosing SMART goals, meaning Specific, Measurable, Achievable, Relevant, and Time-limited.

Why it's challenging or meaningful: why would achieving the goal matter to you and other people involved?

Cooking dinner and asking someone else to set the table isn't that challenging. Organizing a dinner party with a speaker might be. Organizing a set of dinners with a revolving set of speakers would likely be. Organizing your three apartment-mates to agree to a plan of rotating chores and responsibilities, where everyone is accountable and getting it to stick would likely be too.

Your role: what do you plan to do to lead the others and to participate in the work of the project?

The roles of the people you'll lead: what other work needs to be done and who is there who can do it? What roles do you envision for each of them, keeping in mind they may not want to do some things.

Accountability: how will you be held accountable to keep you motivated?

What success means in this project: how will you know you've finished? How will you feel when you've finished? How will your teammates feel?

What failure means in this project: how will you know if you should change the project or give up?

EXERCISE CHECKLIST

- ❏ Is your goal smart?
- ❏ Do you care about achieving your goal?
- ❏ Will your project require you to lead at least one other person?
- ❏ Does your project have clear signs of success or failure so you don't work on it forever?

 Stop reading. Put the book down and do the exercise.

REFLECTION QUESTIONS

I recommend reflecting on your experience with this chapter's exercise before continuing. You can reflect about anything you found relevant, but here are some questions you may want to consider:

♦ Do you care about your goal?
♦ How do you feel about taking on the challenge . . . anxious? excited? nervous? other?
♦ How do you feel about being held accountable for the goal to other people?
♦ Do you have access to people who can help you achieve the goal?
♦ How do you feel about leading others?
♦ How will having the skills of leading and inspiring others change your career and life?

Post-Exercise

Have you ever prepared for a leadership interaction, like a negotiation or interview, and thought, "I'm prepared! I'm going to say X, they'll say Y, I'll say Z, they'll agree, and it will come out great!"? Then you open the door, see the other people, everything you prepared flies out of your head, and you feel like you didn't prepare at all?

That's the difference between knowing what to do in theory or academically versus in practice or from experience. Method Learning prepares you with practice and experience. Even so, we've mostly been leading ourselves so far. Leading others challenges you emotionally and socially beyond leading yourself. Creating a project that you care about where you lead people you care about lets you face those challenges on your terms so when you face them elsewhere in life, you can fall back on your experience from these exercises.

Doing Unit 4's exercises with family and friends helps you develop their skills with people who support you, which gets you started. Doing them on a project you're accountable for increases that challenge and bridges the gap to doing them on other people's terms.

Before continuing, I recommend ensuring your project is not too easy or too hard for you. If you do, you will remember and use the next few exercises and their application for the rest of your career and life.

Leading Others

Unit 4: Leading Others focuses on leading through empathy, compassion, listening, and supportive management that avoids micromanagement.

This unit is the culmination of all of the preceding exercises. You will learn to behave and communicate to attract others to your teams and then to inspire them to find meaning, value, importance, and purpose in their work. They will want to work effectively, produce quality, feel ownership, and thank you for it.

CHAPTER 17

Meaningful Connection

If someone you've dreamed of meeting walked into the room, would you be prepared to start a conversation with him or her? Would you know how to meaningfully connect, or would you just say what came to mind and hope for the best?

I've asked this question of hundreds of students and workshop participants, and none offered a consistent, reliable, predictable approach for this common, important situation. The most common suggestion is to break the ice with "Hi, how are you?" or "So, what do you do?" and hope for commonalities to base a conversation on. In other words, even rooms full of MBAs and seasoned executives have no better plan than I did with the author at the panel and probably end up like Beth at the Armory, not approaching.

Frances Hesselbein was such a contact for me. What did I do that worked with her that didn't with the author? To refresh your memory, with the author, I introduced myself, hoped for the best, and got nowhere, like with many meetings for most of my life to that point.

Yet with no more academic training, a few years later, in my first conversation with Frances Hesselbein, I turned our scheduled 30-minute coffee into a deep conversation over lunch. I could have been intimidated by her office's gleaming swords and pictures of her with presidents. Instead I felt comfortable, and she remarked,

"I don't remember a more delightful conversation," and later made several high-level professional introductions for me.

What made the difference is that I had practiced making meaningful connections—again, that's *practiced*, not read about, analyzed, or debated case studies on. Business school taught *about* networking. Practice meant that when her assistant sat me down and Frances asked, "So, what do you want to talk about?" I responded based on experience.

I said, "I understand leadership is a passion of yours. Is that right?"

She said it was.

I said, "Cool . . . You know Marshall loves leadership. He coaches. He tells me that it's about helping people make positive long-term changes in their behavior. I love to lead, too, especially teaching. For me, it's enabling people to create meaning, value, importance, and purpose in their lives and those people around them. What is leading for you?"

Without pausing, she said, "To serve is to live."

I said, "Wow, that says a lot. 'To serve . . . A lot of people think of leaders as telling others what to do, like leaders are above their followers. 'To serve' sounds like the opposite. Can you clarify why you specify 'to serve'?"

She responded at length, describing what service meant in the context of leadership. I asked a few questions to clarify.

When she finished talking about service, I asked, "When you say 'to live,' you sound like leadership to you is about more than just business. What do you mean by 'to live'?"

She responded at length again, describing how much leadership connected with other parts of life.

From there we continued talking about leadership and life.

Creating *Meaningful Connections*

I don't mind if the conversation fragment I just recounted sounded unremarkable, since my goal isn't to wow people. It's to make my conversational counterpart and myself feel comfortable opening up and feeling supported. I followed a script-based structure that I call *Meaningful Connection*. I use it regularly to create meaningful connections and have taught it to hundreds of students and clients.

Michelle Lands an Interview: *Meaningful Connection* Beats a Résumé

Michelle was my first student to jump for joy in class—during a field trip to a job fair where she practiced *Meaningful Connection*.

She had come to NYU, where she took my class, from Mexico to get a master's degree in design and technology. The class was in entrepreneurial marketing and sales. I organized a class trip to a job fair, framing a job search as entrepreneurially marketing and selling your labor.

Before the class trip, to gauge their willingness to try this approach, I asked if they went to job fairs.

"No," they all agreed.

"Why not?" I asked.

One explained, "They just take your résumé and tell you to apply online. What's the point?"

"Were any of you going to apply to any of the companies coming to this fair?" I asked.

Nobody was.

I asked, "Have any of you hired someone and found them to be a great employee?"

Some had.

I continued, "Have any of you loved any of your jobs?"

Some had.

I continued, "What did you like about the hires and jobs you liked?"

Those with experience said they liked the hires for things like being conscientious and caring about their work. They liked their jobs for things like being challenged and effective managers.

"Did any of those qualities show up on the résumés or job descriptions?"

They paused before answering. They agreed, "No."

"So if the résumés and job descriptions didn't tell you what mattered, do you have anything to lose in leaving your business cards and résumés at home and talking to the reps in a different way?"

They sat up in their seats at this question. They seemed to get my point, that they had nothing to lose in experimenting. I introduced *Meaningful Connection* and we spent half a class learning and practicing the exercise. At the job fair, I assigned them to practice it with the reps instead of trading résumés for business cards.

Before talking to her first rep, Michelle asked, "None of the companies are looking for designers. What should I do?"

"Then you have the most freedom," I said. "Practice with anyone and see what happens."

She disappeared into the crowd while I helped other students.

Ten minutes later she ran back, jumping and smiling. "I got an invitation! I did it, I got an interview!"

She explained that she only did *Meaningful Connection*. The exercise forced her to listen to the reps and talk to them as people, not positions on organization charts. Instead of promoting herself, she had to listen and connect.

The rep told her why he invited her to the interview: "We wrote on the brochure that we wanted programmers because we expected only programmers here. But we want people who 'get it' more than anything, and you seem to. We can teach work skills if you need them, but we can't teach 'getting it.'" Ironic that I had taught her just that.

The *Meaningful Connection* Exercise

Some people wonder about using a prepared conversation structure—a script. I care about the person and what they say, not the originality of the conversation structure. Shakespeare's sonnets were no less meaningful and expressive for their rigid structure. I want a structure that allows the other person and their meaning to come out. *Meaningful Connection* consistently leads to unique, personal, meaningful, two-way conversation content, even if the structure doesn't change.

Practicing it makes me more comfortable and confident and helps me focus on the other person. That confidence means we talk less about traffic, weather, and other meaningless small talk and more about subjects we care about. I wonder less what to say. I enjoy learning about the person. People seem more open, less guarded, and more engaged. I talk to more people than I would otherwise.

Meaningful Connection is useful in networking, job interviews, social events, and any team context. I use it weekly or more, sometimes several times a day. It's not the only way to create a meaningful connection, but it works. Practicing it reveals its underlying structure and skills that you'll use in meeting and leading others. It's also the foundation for all the exercises in Unit 4, Leading Others.

You can do *Meaningful Connection* in a few minutes or, with practice, you can extend it to full conversations, as I did with Frances. You can do it once or you can do it two or three times in a row. You can do it with people you know well or just met, with friends, family, coworkers, classmates, and so on. You don't have to tell people you're doing an exercise.

What to Do

Practice the script below at least a dozen times one way (you do the odd steps) and a few times the other (they do the odd steps). In university, I assign students to do it twice a day for a week.

The first few times you do it will take a lot of concentration, especially thinking of two people for step 3 and remembering the words in step 4 to use in step 5, but it gets easier with a few tries. Even Meryl Streep has to learn and practice her lines. Unlike her, you don't have to create a character with a fictional back story. You only have to be you. You can show people the script while you do it the first time if it helps.

The Script

1. Ask their passion, or what they like to do, besides work and family.
2. They will reply with something still fairly usual: travel, books, food, and so on.
3. Say "Cool. . . . You know, I know [*someone you know*] who [*does X*] for [*their reason*] and I know [*someone else*] who [*does X*] for [*their reason*]. Why do you [*do X*]?"
4. Their response will include two or three words that are unusual or stressed.
5. Respond to clarify what they said using those two or three words in your response.

You don't have to make time to do the exercise, since you can do it in regular conversation, with people you've just met, people you've known a long time, and everyone between.

Example

Someone doing *Meaningful Connection* with me might get a conversation like this:

PERSON: "Hey, Josh. If you don't mind my asking, what's a passion of yours, besides work and family?"

ME: "Hmm . . . I like running marathons."

PERSON: "Cool . . . You know, I know a few people who exercise a lot. My brother runs a lot. I think he does it since he loved running track in school and likes to keep up the habit with a track club. My coworker works with a trainer at her gym. I think she mainly does it to keep in shape. Why do you run marathons?"

ME: "It's not really those things, though I did do sports in school. And I'm not sure running marathons is actually that healthy. For me, it's more about discipline, since running far is so hard. I don't run with a group. There's something about the solitude I like, learning about myself."

PERSON, having noticed the word *discipline*: "So, it's more about discipline?"

ME: "Yeah. Like after running up a big hill in 90-degree weather 16 miles in, dealing with difficult people in the rest of life isn't so hard. . . ."

I could talk a lot about the discipline I've developed from exercise, especially endurance sports. Even writing right now, I want to. After I did, the other person might continue. . . .

PERSON, having noticed the word *solitude*: "So there's something about running in solitude that you like?"

ME: "Yeah, running takes almost no equipment. Just shoes and clothes and I can run in Central Park or by the Hudson

River and not have to worry about anything else for a
while. . . ."

Discussion

Some people consider "So what do you do?" a standard way to start
a conversation. I find it distracts from more meaningful topics. The
same with weather, sports, where they're from, current events,
traffic on the way over, how many siblings they have, and the other
topics people fall back on. They're standard scripts we don't think
of as scripts because we're so used to them. They aren't *bad*. They
just create little intimacy or meaning. They're standard *because*
they prevent sharing or exposing vulnerabilities. The problem with
avoiding vulnerabilities is that we're vulnerable about things we
care about, so using them also avoids what we care about. I suggest
saying "besides work and family" not because people don't care
about them but because they tend to get stock answers, again to
avoid vulnerabilities.

People also fall back on standard questions because they don't
have alternatives that work, which this exercise gives.

Sharing about passions makes people vulnerable and open to
being judged, manipulated, used, or otherwise hurt, which tends to
discourage them from speaking. To motivate them to speak, you
have to lead them to feel safe. Saying you won't judge (or manipu-
late, etc) isn't credible because people who do also say they won't.
This exercise shows that you won't judge through your behavior,
which is more credible than words, which gives them space to open
up. The script keeps you from talking over them, judging them, interviewing them, or falling into mundane conversation.

Meaningful Connection makes other people feel comfortable sharing something they care about. Most likely in step 2 they will give a
cocktail-party answer—a protective facade hiding a deeper passion.
You connecting their answer to people in your life in step 3 supports

them, which leads them to expand. People *want* to talk about their passions. In fact, they love to, just not when they feel vulnerable. They do when they feel supported.

I recommend first practicing the two hard parts with people you know well—connecting to people you know and their motivations in step 3 and listening for their meaning-carrying words in step 4. I also recommend following the script until you master it, which usually takes about 10 trials. You have the rest of your life to add flourishes and improvise. Playing *do re mi fa so la ti do* will teach you about scales, not *do fa re mi ti la so do*. The goal of doing the exercise so consistently at first is not for you to do it the same way forever but to master the basics so you don't have to think about them. Then your natural voice will emerge.

The Word *Passion*

Students often ask if using the word *passion* is appropriate in professional contexts, where some say they feel uncomfortable saying it. I can tell from their tones that they'd feel uncomfortable using it in casual contexts, too. I suggest a few points.

First, you don't need to use it if you don't want. You can ask "What are your hobbies besides work and family?", "What do you like doing besides work and family?," or variations like that.

Second, I point out that I felt uncomfortable asking about passions at first, too. I soon found it the most effective word. No one has ever suggested I did something wrong asking them. So while it isn't required, I recommend trying it. Past students report that they grew into it, too. Quoting a reflection from a participant in the online version of this course, an entrepreneur who had sold a software business,

At first I felt weird about using the word *passion*, but not any more. I mean why? Everyone wants passion, so why would it be

weird to say. Sometimes I got a response like "Ehm, my passion?" like "Passion? Really?", but when they saw I was being se-
rious and sincere that changed to something that looked like
"Well, maybe I do have a passion" and then they would start
talking happily.

These experiences really deepen the belief that people are
just like me, in the sense that our emotions and minds work the
same way at least.

The change is more dramatic during workshops I lead on *Meaningful Connection* in companies where participants know each other.
Before doing the exercise, participants ask a lot about using the
word. After, they talk about their pleasant surprise at learning
things for the first time about people they'd worked with for years,
and how comfortable it felt to share.

Third, I rhetorically ask them if they want more passion in their
life and how much they expect if they can't even use the word. Then
I ask, more positively, if they start using the word, would they expect to develop more passion and connect with more passionate
people?

Regarding the word's appropriateness in professional contexts, I
tell about a client's friend who had lunch with Warren Buffett,
whom I consider reasonably for a professional. The client's friend
wrote about the experience,

> Throughout the conversation, Buffett stressed the significance
> of passion—how necessary it was for his own journey and how
> imperative it is for us to find ours. Passion was the fire behind
> his focus that encouraged him to absorb all things business, all
> the time. It was a job, it was his life.

You might say Buffett can talk about passion because he's so successful. I suggest that he is so successful because he talks about passion.

So use the word or alternatives as you feel comfortable, but I suggest trying it for the experience.

Meaning-Carrying Words

Words can't express our thoughts, emotions, and meaning, as we found in *Inner Monologue*. The meaning and emotions words can't express all of come out in our nonverbal communication around the words, usually through gestures, volume, facial expression, eye contact, unusual word choice, and so on. When you use the word they attached that nonverbal communication to, they will hear that meaning, even beyond what you may have sensed. Ask how people feel when you use their meaning-carrying words. I do in workshops. and the overwhelmingly most common answers are "I felt listened to" and "I felt you understood me."

What Not to Do

A common mistake I see after someone shares his or her passion is for the student to ask him or her to expand on it in step 3, such as in the following:

YOU (STEP 1): "What's your passion?"

PERSON (STEP 2): "I love traveling."

YOU (NOT STEP 3): "What about traveling do you like?" or "Really, why?"

There's nothing *wrong* with asking someone "why" in other conversations, but *Meaningful Connection* practices specific skills. Asking "why" can lead to enjoyable conversations, but anyone who has had a child ask "Why? . . . Why? . . . Why? . . . Why? . . . ?" knows it can make other people feel like they're doing all the work, like they're being interviewed. To share a passion makes them vulnerable, so asking for more information can make them feel more vulnerable, leading them to share less.

I'm not saying to stop the conversations you're used to forever, just to follow the script when practicing *Meaningful Connection* so you'll learn experientially.

The exercise also keeps you from talking over the other person, as in,

YOU (STEP 1): "What's your passion?"

PERSON (STEP 2): "Traveling."

YOU (NOT STEP 3): "Really? Me too. I love traveling. I just got back from Paris. Let me tell you about the trip. It was awesome. . . ."

Talking over them will make many people feel like you asked them to share as an excuse to talk about yourself. Then they'll share less, compete to talk back over you, or withdraw in other ways. They won't likely feel listened to or meaningfully connected.

Avoid doing something else I used to do: I would try to show I was listening by translating their message into my language. It sounds great but does the opposite. Why? Because it keeps you from using their meaning-carrying words.

If you *don't* use their words, they'll feel like you don't understand or weren't listening, which feels frustrating to them. For example, if they say they love cooking because "It's like composing a *symphony* for your senses," and you say, "So it's like writing a *song* for your senses," they'll likely feel, "No, if I felt like it was a song, I would have said 'song.' I meant symphony." If you're lucky they'll explain the difference, but they'll more likely wonder, "Why bother talking about something important if you aren't listening?"

Having someone do *Meaningful Connection* with you, where they do the odd steps, which I assign as part of this chapter, lets you experience the other side. In my experience, it feels great. I like feeling listened to—no less for knowing they're using a script. Another useful variation is to have a friend purposefully use the wrong words in steps 3 and 5 for you to feel that frustration.

Again, I recommend sticking with the script until you've mastered it. The more you master the basics, the more skillfully you'll improvise and the sooner your voice will emerge.

Why a Script?

I didn't invent the idea of using a script to creat,e authenticity, openness, and confidence. I adapted it from two of the most effective sources for learning such skills I found. The first was actors and other performers, who learn from scripts, musical scores, choreographed routines, and so on. Meryl Streep is more authentic for following a script, not less. John Coltrane didn't play random notes. He followed a score based on a structure. Athletes run plays. Only by practicing the structure can performers express themselves freely, even—or especially—to improvise.

Even improvisational performers who don't use scripts follow script-like structures. *Meaningful Connection* is between a script and an improvisational structure, which I call a *script* for convenience. The second source was Marshall Goldsmith and his techniques, especially his script-based *Feedforward*.

Scripts take care of a conversation's structure so you can focus on yourself and the other person. Before practicing acting exercises and *Feedforward*, I might have considered scripts fake for making me use other people's words. Then I saw how effectively they enable you to express yourself genuinely and authentically. It's time mainstream leadership education adopted them.

I also noticed how many preset scripts most people already use: "Hi, how are you?" is part of a script. So are "My name is Josh," "So, where are you from?," "So, what do you do?," and "Where did you go to school?" Read enough of my blog and you'll develop that disdain for meaningless small talk as I learned which conversational elements led to meaningful conversations and which didn't. Weather, sports, and traffic on the way over didn't. People's motivations, passions, and nonverbal communication did. Since many aspiring leaders aren't yet comfortable sharing their vulnerabilities, scripts also enable them to practice new communication modes they might not otherwise know how to.

The question isn't whether to use scripts or not but which to use—ones that create meaning or ones that bore people and lead them to put up facades.

EXERCISE CHECKLIST

- ❏ Did you do the exercise at least a dozen times?
- ❏ Did you have someone do the script back to you?
- ❏ Did you follow the script for at least the first 5 or 10 times?
- ❏ Did you pay attention to the other person's reaction?
- ❏ Did you pay attention to your reaction?
- ❏ Did you look for ways to improve each time?

 Stop reading. Put the book down and do the exercise.

REFLECTION QUESTIONS

I recommend reflecting on your experience with this
chapter's exercise before continuing. You can reflect about
anything you found relevant, but here are some questions
you may want to consider:

- How did you feel using someone else's words?
- Are other greetings scripts?
- How did your experience and results change with
  practice?
- How do you feel about "So, what do you do?"; traffic;
  weather; and other common greetings?
- How would you approach someone you've never met
  before?
- How do you feel about talking about people's
  passions?
- Where and how might you apply your experience in
  the rest of your life?

Post-Exercise

The Dalai Lama, waiting one morning for a hotel elevator to leave
for a conference, spoke a few words to a maid working in the hall.
She said a few words back, looking very happy for the attention.
The next morning, he left at the same time. The same maid was
there again, this time with a coworker. They spoke a few words and
both maids looked very happy. By the end of his stay, half the hotel
staff formed a receiving line to meet him.

It doesn't take much to connect—just to treat someone like a human. When you do, they respond, often a lot. Sadly, our society doesn't treat people like humans that much.

Meaningful Connection has changed how I meet people and my default depth of relationship. Now I expect to connect meaningfully when I meet, at least when I want to. I'm confident meeting new people independent of their status—higher or lower. I haven't reached the Dalai Lama's level of empathy and compassion yet, but I believe I meet people as people, not positions on organization charts. The basis for my relationships is MVIP because I know how to create it. I can't describe how much of an improvement it's made to my relationships and life.

I often say that before learning to lead, my life was about facts, knowledge, and rules—a rat race—and now it's about relationships and emotions and that nearly every relationship today is better than nearly any before. The skills *Meaningful Connection* builds are probably the biggest factor in that improvement.

While I don't claim to be the world's greatest conversationalist, people often ask if I was born as outgoing as I am and sound surprised to hear my anecdotes about flubbing. There are many more than with the author on the panel. The change took years of time and work. I'm still doing it. Since I use *The Method*, though, that process is rewarding.

Have you seen a skilled salsa dancer lead a partner in an incredible spin move and asked how to do it? It looks like it's in the hands, but they tell me it's in the feet—what you learn in the first lesson. Great musicians, dancers, and other performers seem to describe their best work as the basics with variations and flourishes. The more I practice *Meaningful Connection*, the more I see it as a leadership basic I can add variations and flourishes to. Sometimes I think of it like a jazz standard that Louis Armstrong might play one way one day, another way another day; Charlie Parker another; Miles Davis another, and so on.

I once saw Brian Dennehy on a panel discussion. An audience

member asked him if he got bored playing *Death of a Salesman's* Willy Loman—a role he won a Tony, an Emmy, and a Lawrence Olivier award playing—hundreds of times. He said, on the contrary, that he learned more about the character with each performance and felt like he was just getting to understand him. Scripts make available that depth, richness, genuineness, and authenticity.

I use *Meaningful Connection* and the skills in it weekly, sometimes daily, and it consistently creates productive, meaningful connections, like Dennehy learning about Loman. I feel like I'm still learning about myself and people in general through it. While it's helpful on its own, it helps yet more in the exercises to come.

I find people enjoy sharing passions more than they expect. Performance in leadership involves other people more directly than in most other ASEEP fields. Great leadership performances make the people you lead active. They thank you for leading them. Sadly, society today seems to value talking more over talking more meaningfully or listening more. You don't have to be the Dalai Lama for those social norms to drive people to you. You only have to connect meaningfully, human to human.

Connecting as humans helps yourself as a leader. As Dwight Eisenhower said,

> In the Army, whenever I became fed up with meetings, protocol, and paperwork, I could rehabilitate myself by a visit with the troops. Among them, talking to each other as individuals, and listening to each other's stories, I was refreshed and could return to headquarters reassured that, hidden behind administrative entanglements, the military was an enterprise manned by human beings.

CHAPTER 18

Make People Feel Understood

Shaquille O'Neal is one of the greatest basketball centers of all time, having led teams to four NBA championships, among other achievements. In seven seasons before 1999, though, he hadn't won a championship. Instead, he was feuding publicly with a teammate, contributing to the team underperforming.

Things changed that season. He won the regular-season Most Valuable Player award. His team won the championship, and the next two, with O'Neal winning the finals MVP all three times. Many compare him favorably to Wilt Chamberlain, another dominant center.

What turned things around in 1999?

A major contribution was the leadership of Phil Jackson, who started coaching O'Neal that year. Jackson had coached many great players to many championships, so he knew how to bring the best out of players. He recounted one way he led O'Neal to greatness:

At one point five games into the season, he's coming off the court, and I stopped him as he's going to the bench and I said, "What was the greatest thing Wilt did in his career?"

"Oh, wow, he scored fifty points a game for an entire season."

I said, "Yeah, that was great, but it's not as great as he played every single minute of every game. . . . Do you think you can do that?"

And he said, "If he did it, I can do it."

So I played him for maybe a week and a half, two weeks forty-eight minutes a game. And he got in really good shape.

[Teammate John] Salley, his emissary, came and said, "You know, Shaq's having second thoughts about playing forty-eight minutes a game. Can you maybe cut him back down to maybe thirty-six, thirty-eight?" And I did.

It was one of the ways I tried to motivate him to really get himself into position for that season. And that was his MVP season. He was a tremendous player that year.

In other words, Jackson motivated O'Neal to play harder than ever—harder than he could maintain beyond two weeks—with enthusiasm and ownership of the effort. Jackson didn't try to convince, debate, or coerce O'Neal.

Instead, Jackson connected O'Neal's passion to compete with Wilt Chamberlain for historical greatness to his task for him to get more fit. O'Neal didn't play harder for Jackson; he did it for himself.

How did Jackson know what passion of O'Neal's to tap into? Today we can speculate that it was easy to know O'Neal's competition with Chamberlain, but hindsight is 20/20. O'Neal could have had other passions, and Jackson tapping something O'Neal didn't care about could have alienated him.

Making people feel understood and comfortable sharing their passions gives leaders powerful tools to lead people with—tools that people *like* being led by. Everyone has strong motivations—what I call passions. If you worked hard to get where you are, then your teammates did, too. They had to get high grades, sacrifice fun, work long hours, handle parental pressure, or whatever challenges they faced and overcame, as you did.

Something motivated them to get there. That passion was there before you met them and will motivate them more than any external incentive you could try to motivate them with. You'll lead people more effectively with their existing passions than by creating new ones. When you do, they will feel ownership and MVIP and want to do the work for themselves. They will feel listened to and appreciated. When you don't, they'll resent you for ignoring them. People who don't feel listened to and appreciated feel compelled to keep talking until they do, which feels like pushing back or insubordination, or they give up on communicating with you. When they don't have to talk so much, they can focus on their work.

This parable illustrates the difference between external incentives and internal motivations:

Some children started playing ball in a park. Next to the park lived an elderly man. He went out on his porch and asked them to play more quietly. They said it was a public park and didn't stop playing.

The old man went inside, came back out, and said to them, "If I can't get you to play more quietly, then I'll give you each one dollar."

The kids were confused but accepted the money and went back to playing, more happy than before for the money.

The next day they came to play again. Again he called them over and gave each a dollar. They kept playing, more happily for the money.

The next day they played and he gave them each a dollar. Again the next day and the next and the next.

Then one day, as they played, they realized he hadn't come out. They knocked on his door.

When he came out, they asked why he hadn't come out and if he had dollars for them.

He said, "I'm sorry, I don't have any more money for you. You'll have to play without the dollars."

So they stopped playing and went home.

The old man knew he could undermine the kids' internal motivations with external incentives. Many managers do what he did without realizing it. They don't know that people have powerful internal motivations so don't bother learning how to learn them. As a result, they don't know how to lead in the most effective way for each person.

The leader's challenge is to get them to share their passions with you. It's a challenge because we've all learned from experience that our passions make us vulnerable, so we protect them. Classmates teased us in school. People manipulated or used us to their advantage. We've had our hearts broken. We get emotionally hurt by what we care about. More caring and passion means more vulnerability.

This chapter's exercise, *Make People Feel Understood*, shows you how to make people feel comfortable sharing their passions in a different way than *Meaningful Connection*. Where *Meaningful Connection* led to conversation and open communication, this exercise leads people to share their passions so they'll feel open to you leadership with these passions.

They will feel understood, which is very different from you feeling you understand them. This difference is worth clarifying: You will make them feel understood, which is different and more valuable in leading them than you feeling you understand them. You understanding them happens in your head. Them feeling understood happens in their heads and hearts. Their heads and hearts motivate them, not yours, no matter what you think should motivate them.

This exercise makes your conversation about motivations, and strong ones in particular. Again, as carpenters work with wood and programmers work with "source code," leaders work with motivations. Not knowing someone's motivations and emotions makes leading them difficult. *Make People Feel Understood* opens people to share their "source code" instead of the usual workplace facade. In time, openness feels more natural for everyone. It feels empathetic, compassionate, and friendly.

As you will see, people feel very good talking about their passions when they know the other person will support them and not judge, laugh at, use, or otherwise hurt them. This exercise enables you to give them that support, credibly and effectively. You will develop the skills of empathy and compassion. You will both feel comfortable with you leading them.

The *Make People Feel Understood* Exercise

Making people feel understood about their passions and then connecting those passions to their work creates for them MVIP in that work. Them feeling misunderstood will make that work feel meaningless, especially if you motivate with money, promotions, demotions, your motivations, or other external incentives that devalue their passions. That lack of MVIP is what people escape when they leave bad managers.

Others' passions aren't obvious. Although a team may have a common goal, people have unique personal motivations. One person may go to college out of a love for learning, another to play sports, another to watch sports. Others' goals may be socializing, getting jobs, family, and so on.

Say you go to school because you love learning but someone assumes you're there to get a job. If they suggest a class because it will get you hired but you won't learn in it, you'll likely feel misunderstood and less likely to follow that person's lead.

The leader's challenge is to lead others to feel you understand them so they feel comfortable sharing their passion and open to you leading them with it.

It takes practice. This exercise's goal is to create the feeling in them of being understood for a passion. We'll build on that skill to lead people in chapter 19's exercise.

What to Do

Practice the script below at least a dozen times one way (you initiating step 1) and a couple times the other way (the other person initiating). In university, I assign students to do it twice a day for a week, like *Meaningful Connection*. You can start with people you know. You can show them the script too at first if it makes it easier, but work up to doing the exercise without it.

The Script

1. Ask, "What's your passion?" or something similar, like, "I can tell you work harder on this than you have to. What's your motivation to care so much?"
2. The person will usually give a cocktail-party answer.
3. Confirm your understanding.
4. *Confirmation/Clarification Cycle*:
   - Let them correct you.
   - Ask confirmation and clarification questions as necessary to refine your understanding.
   - Confirm your new understanding.
   - Repeat to *Universal Emotion* (see below).

Note that the exercise requires paying closer attention to the motivations the person describes than to the behavior he or she describes.

Example

Someone doing *Make People Feel Understood* with me might go like this:

PERSON: "You seem to like teaching leadership. What's your passion there?"

ME: "Yeah, I do. Before I learned it, I thought I led well, but looking back, I made a lot of mistakes. I didn't realize how important relationships were."

PERSON: "So you like teaching leadership because of what you learned about how important relationships were?"

ME: "Yeah. When I started my first company, my background was science and analysis, not emotions and relationships."

PERSON: "So leadership moved you from analysis to relationships?"

ME: "Exactly. I often say that nearly all of my relationships now are better than nearly any of them before. A lot of what I teach is how to make relationships more enjoyable and productive in give-and-take contexts like business. I think a lot of people are like I was and would benefit from developing like I did, only a lot faster."

PERSON: "So teaching leadership is a lot about your growing and learning?"

ME: "Exactly. I think all leaders constantly develop themselves. This is one way I'm doing it. Teaching and coaching have helped me grow more than I ever would have imagined."

Note how PERSON's questions simply ask clarification or confirmation, not adding new information or asking for elaboration, and how my responses get longer and more personal each time. This pattern is typical of this exercise.

The script introduces two new concepts: the *Confirmation/Clarification Cycle* and the *Universal Emotion*. I'll explain them below, but practicing the exercise teaches them best.

The Universal Emotion

The Universal Emotion is one of the core concepts of this book's progression of exercises. It is an emotion and motivation that anyone at any time in any culture would recognize. It makes empathizing easy when you know how to make people feel comfortable sharing their feelings. Like any vulnerability, people protect it.

An example that is not a Universal Emotion is if you ask people why they work so hard or care so much about a task and they say they do it for the money. There are cultures that don't use money. We've been human for hundreds of thousands of years but have had money for maybe a tenth of that time. So, to make money is not universal. On the contrary, we value money as a placeholder for universal things.

Nearly every first answer people give about their passions and motivations is a cocktail-party answer—comfortable and acceptable while hinting at deeper motivations. Since we've all been hurt, used, laughed at, humiliated, brokenhearted, and so on, we have learned that greater pain comes with greater openness about stronger motivations. We've learned to protect our emotions, usually by not sharing them. Sometimes we make light of them or act as if we don't care, but we all care about some things deeply.

You reading this book means you care about your work, relationships, and emotional well-being. You worked hard to reach where you are—you took risks, worked late, put off fun, challenged yourself, or made what looked like sacrifices to others but you saw as investments. You may be only vaguely aware of what deep motivations are keeping you going, but they are there. Your hard work means you are also surrounded by people who have worked as hard or overcome comparable challenges, motivated by equally strong emotions.

These strong emotions will motivate people more than any motivation you could layer on top. In fact, motivating people by other means will imply you don't value their motivations. You neglecting their passions will feel to them like you imposing your values on them, which we learned to avoid in Unit 2. They will also feel like the kids the old man discouraged from playing ball by giving them dollars. People whose passions you neglect will feel like you're dismissing or overriding their internal motivations with external incentives. Not connecting their passions—their Universal Emotions—to their work deprives them of MVIP in their work and contributes to them feeling like they joined a good company with bad managers.

Later chapters will describe how to lead people with their Universal Emotions. For now our goal is to make people feel comfortable sharing them. We do so with the Confirmation/Clarification Cycle.

The Confirmation/Clarification Cycle

The Confirmation/Clarification Cycle is a deceptively simple technique to make people feel comfortable sharing their vulnerabilities with you and is as effective for what it doesn't do.

What it does is have you confirm and clarify your understanding of their motivations iteratively, leading them to share more each time, in a way that makes them feel good. It works because people love sharing their motivations when they expect the listener will support them. *Meaningful Connection* achieves this goal by showing them you support people like them in your world. The Confirmation/Clarification Cycle does it by consistently putting their interests before yours.

Once you ask about people's passion or strong motivation, they think of it, putting it in their thoughts for a while. They want to talk about it. They also want to protect it. Trying to increase their motivation to share rarely overcomes their protection since talking about passions is already a high motivation. You can't increase it much. Decreasing their protection works more. Instead of pushing them harder over the wall, lower the wall. Simply saying you'll support and won't judge or hurt them isn't credible to people who don't already know you well because people who would hurt them would say the same thing.

The Confirmation/Clarification Cycle works like this.

The first time people tell you of a passion, they share only part of it, the cocktail-party answer. You confirming your understanding will sound wrong to them, no matter how accurately you repeat what they said. Unless your nonverbal communication is objectionable, they'll correct you. Most people, on being corrected, feel they got it wrong and move on to other topics. In the Confirmation/Clarification Cycle, you *expect* them to correct you. You know that even if you repeated their words perfectly, your words could never match their thoughts. Your goal isn't to restate them perfectly. The exercise is 95 percent to make them feel comfortable sharing and 5 percent for you to understand. Leadership is about them, not you.

Next, respond to their correction by refining your understanding and confirming your new understanding. Each time they hear you put their communication and interests before yours, they feel more comfortable to share more. Words are cheap. You show through your behavior that you care about what they say. The barrier that protects their Universal Emotion lowers, and they eventually share it.

Note what the cycle prevents you from doing. It prevents you from talking over them, interviewing them, injecting your points or judgment, changing the subject, judging them, or anything besides showing you care about understanding them.

Before doing it, many students ask if it's pushy to ask similar questions over and over. On the contrary, for the person being asked, it feels like you care about her (I assign doing the exercise in both directions for you to experience this feeling). It puts the other person's interests first.

The cycle will give you a strong, unmistakable feeling that you understand the other person on something deeply important to them. You'll feel interested in their passion. (One of the reasons you'll never tire of the exercise is the unique interest each person's passion creates.) They'll talk with increasing openness and enthusiasm. They'll show appreciation for your insight, listening, and persistence. You'll also sense the feeling evaporate if you deviate from the script, and digress from their interest and put yourself first.

For example, people might first say that they like their work because it pays the bills. Since there are many cultures without bills, you haven't reached a Universal Emotion so you'd continue with the Confirmation/Clarification Cycle. They might then say they want to get rich. Again, there are cultures without money, so you'd keep clarifying and confirming. If they then said that they want to give their children a happy life, I'd say that sounds like a Universal Emotion. Now you'd know one of the passions driving them.

Reaching and stating a Universal Emotion often leads people to personal insights, often deep. They may feel an epiphany and thank you for it or for connecting parts of their lives they hadn't before, as if you had seen an insight that prompted you to persist with the cycle. They don't know that you followed a structure. They tend to conclude that you persisted because you saw something below their surface that was meaningful enough to put your interests aside.

Nonverbal communication and body language play a big role with the Universal Emotion. You will almost always see several clear changes when you reach their Universal Emotion: They will lean forward to talk and their face will light up. They will also tend to switch from short, reserved, protective answers to longer, expressive, explanatory answers. You'll sense that they suddenly want to share something they want to but rarely get to, like, "*Finally*, I can tell someone why I'm *really* doing this!"

You'll probably note feelings in yourself of understanding and also something like, "I bet if I led the person with this, I could get them to do a lot more." You may have a Machiavellian feeling that you could use this insight to your advantage but also a compassionate feeling that you wouldn't.

Is Evoking Their Passions Prying or Too Personal?

People often ask if the technique is too personal for the workplace. Learning experientially works best here. After you've seen a few people share Universal Emotions, you see how much people love it and learn about themselves. Even more, after someone leads you to some Universal Emotions of your own, you'll feel how liberating, comfortable, satisfying, and friendly it feels.

EXERCISE CHECKLIST

- ❑ Did you do the exercise at least a dozen times?
- ❑ Did you have someone do the script back to you?
- ❑ Did you follow the script for at least the first 5 or 10 times?
- ❑ Did you pay attention to the other person's reaction?
- ❑ Did you pay attention to your reaction?
- ❑ Did you look for ways to improve each time?

Stop reading. Put the book down and do the exercise.

REFLECTION QUESTIONS

I recommend reflecting on your experience with this chapter's exercise before continuing. You can reflect about anything you found relevant, but here are some questions you may want to consider:

- How did you feel using someone else's words?
- How did your experience and results change with practice?
- How do you feel about talking about people's passions?
- What do you think about the concept of Universal Emotions?
- How did you feel seeing people share their passions?
- During the Confirmation/Clarification Cycle did you only confirm and clarify without talking about yourself or injecting other new information?
- Where and how might you apply your experience in the rest of your life?

Post-Exercise

Make People Feel Understood has transformed my life, relationships, and emotional awareness as much as *Meaningful Connection*. Connecting on passions instead of facades improves everything from fleeting interactions to my most important long-term relationships. Putting others' interests first is humbling, which helps me learn, grow, and lead.

The feeling *Make People Feel Understood* gives people—feeling understood, being on the receiving end of empathy, compassion, and understanding, and knowing it—is incredibly powerful. Empathy, compassion, and understanding are valuable for leading, but *you* feel them, not the people you're leading, and your feelings don't influence others. *Make People Feel Understood* creates, or rather reveals or unleashes, emotions in others, which motivates them, which means you're leading them. I compare the emotion of feeling understood with love, which society values among the most powerful desired emotions, maybe the most. The more I see of the emotion of feeling understood, the more I see it to be as powerful and meaningful as love. The emotion doesn't have a name and I think we'd benefit from naming it, which I believe would create a lot more empathy in the world.

I can speak from experience of people doing *Make People Feel Understood* with me in workshops many times. Even knowing they're following a script with a room of people watching, it feels good to open up about a passion and feel understood and supported for it. You feel connected and look up to the person who evoked the feeling. You feel liberated and grateful to him or her.

The emotion's opposite—feeling misunderstood—is as important for leaders to know about. Since people communicate to be understood, people who feel misunderstood about something they care about will talk at you until they feel understood or give up, destroying your ability to lead them. Being able to make them feel understood enables you to lead them. Again, I distinguish making them feel understood from understanding them.

I recommend not telling someone, "I understand you," especially when they seem to feel misunderstood. You risk your credibility by setting an impossible standard for yourself since you can't understand others as well as they understand themselves. If you say you understand them and then do something they wouldn't expect you to do if you did, they may see you as confused, lying, or the like. If you feel compelled to tell them you understand them, I recommend saying instead, "If I understand you right . . ." or "Let me see if I understand you . . ." and then confirming your understanding. Still expect them to correct you. You can't put their thoughts and feelings into your words. More effective is to do *Make People Feel Understood* until they say, "*Yes!* You understand me."

You'll be amazed by how many arguments and how much turnover and lost loyalty arise from people not feeling understood. Since emotions get intense when people don't know how to achieve their goals, depriving someone of feeling understood can escalate minor misunderstandings without limit. People feeling misunderstood have to keep talking to make themselves feel understood, escalate to yelling, or give up. If you have authority over them, they may instead silently resent you, protect their vulnerabilities for good, withdraw, and start looking for work elsewhere. If you want to break up with someone but don't want to initiate, intentionally misunderstand them. Do it enough and they'll want to initiate breaking up.

Creating in others the emotion of feeling understood overcomes facades and protections. The more deeply people and teams overcome such barriers, the more closely, effectively, and productively they work, the higher their morale and satisfaction, and the more they support each other, in addition to other benefits.

You'll also be surprised by the conflicts you can resolve or diffuse with *Make People Feel Understood*. You can apply it the same way I suggested using *Feedforward* to resolve arguments. It would have worked in the example with my girlfriend on Sixth Avenue.

The challenge is having the presence of mind to overcome your feelings of self-righteousness or whatever is motivating you to argue. That presence of mind, followed by using an effective technique, puts you in the leadership role, with them responding to you.

By the way, people are motivated by more than one Universal Emotion. You can do the exercise multiple times with the same person. Doing so is effective. It makes him or her feel good; makes the relationship deeper, richer, and more complex; and gives you more tools to lead him or her with.

In the next exercises we'll attach people's passions to tasks, which will make their work feel meaningful. We love leaders who make our work feel meaningful.

For now, I hope you start to abandon the relative superficiality of talking about the weather, sports, current events, and other topics that avoid what people care about. And that you feel more skilled and comfortable at making people feel understood about things they care about.

CHAPTER 19

Lead with Empathy

Chris loves selling. He's the only person I've heard of who chose to take a retail sales job not because he needed the money but to practice his sales skills.

He also did the exercises in this book, as you are doing. He's in his late 20s, finished college, and is the consummate self-starter. He would never settle down into a desk job working for someone else. He loves helping customers directly.

When he started the exercises, cold calling was a basic part of his business's sales process. He had started cold calling on the advice of a mentor he trusted and valued. Despite some early success, by the time he did this book's exercises, he found cold calling frustrating and unproductive. Still, he continued to do it several times a week. He had to force himself to, steeling his nerves to handle the inevitable rejection that never stopped hurting.

The Method in Unit 3 led him to reconsider the beliefs he got from his mentor and conclude that they had stopped working for him. He then used *The Method* to move cold calling out of his life. Based on his success selling in person, he decided to shift to in-person marketing—specifically seminars. Most people fear public speaking, but he had experience there and looked forward to it. He hadn't booked a room, promoted an event, or done other event-planning and marketing tasks, so those parts became his challenge.

The exercises led him to make things happen. *Meaningful Con-*

nection steered him to see people in his community and beyond as more approachable. *Make People Feel Understood* motivated him to talk to people to learn how they wanted to be led and sold.

He began practicing this chapter's exercise, *Lead with Empathy*, to lead his retail coworkers to improve their selling with their passions—their equivalents of Shaquille O'Neal competing with Wilt Chamberlain. One coworker's Universal Emotion was to find beauty in the world, and Chris showed him a beauty in satisfying a customer that he had never seen before. Another had a passion for history, and Chris showed him how sharing history helped create influential relationships. His coworkers' sales went up, and they praised him to the store managers. He also practiced *Lead with Empathy* with his managers, developing peer relationships with them despite their authority over him. He practiced with customers, learning their needs better and upselling them to products that satisfied them more.

Retail was for practice, though. His passion was to start giving seminars.

First he needed a room. He visited a nearby event space and did *Lead with Empathy* with the owner. He wanted the owner to give him a deal on the room. Instead of starting an impersonal transaction, Chris asked the owner what his passion was. The conversation began about coffee (his cocktail-party answer) and then deepened to the owner discussing what life was about for him (his Universal Emotion)—in his words, being one with nature, outside the city, in the wilderness, hiking and fishing. Chris then connected this passion to Chris's task of giving him a deal on the room. Specifically, instead of asking for terms to rent the space, Chris proposed giving him a deal that would help him get out in the wilderness more.

Despite Chris starting vaguely, the owner brightened at Chris's understanding of what he cared about—the wilderness. They talked in terms of helping each other achieve their goals instead of the dollars and cents of renting a space. The owner offered Chris discounts, flexibility, and more. Chris offered to share his revenue. Chris booked the room, they enjoyed working together, and they both felt that they were getting a better deal than usual.

Chris told me that had he known how pleased *Lead with Empathy* would make both parties, he would have used it earlier and more assertively.

Chris and Mark, the Event-Marketing Pro

The next time came soon. Chris needed to fill the seats for the seminar. He remembered an acquaintance he hadn't seen in years, Mark, who worked in event marketing at a Fortune 100 company. Chris's success with the event space owner gave him confidence to approach Mark to do *Lead with Empathy*. His task was to get Mark to help him market his first seminar. As a result of his success with the event space owner, instead of feeling like he was asking a favor, he expected to bring out Mark's relevant passions and help him act on them with his project.

They met over dinner. After catching up, Chris asked Mark what his passion was. Mark started talking about playing drums, but the Confirmation/Clarification Cycle revealed that Mark loved *teaching* drums, which in his words meant creating things and making progress. Mark enjoyed opening up about those passions, as if he hadn't gotten to talk about them in too long.

Chris saw that Mark's job no longer connected his passions to his work, despite his six-figure salary, or more likely because of it, like the old man giving the kids dollars. He also saw that connecting Mark's words—"teaching," "creating things," and "making progress"—to his project would motivate him. So Chris said that he had a project with opportunities for those things using those words. Mark was intrigued and engaged and asked to know more. Chris described his project and needs in Mark's language.

Mark became enthusiastic about helping Chris, which he saw as enabling a friend to implement his passions. In Mark's view, he was probably "teaching" a friend to "create something" and "make progress."

They started collaborating. Beyond helping plan and promote *one* event, Mark taught Chris his practice to plan and promote *events in general*. In fact, he did it for free. Why not? He enjoyed it.

Did Mark feel used, giving freely what his employer paid him for? On the contrary, he loved the project. In fact, Chris told me that Mark felt liberated and enjoyed working with him for free more than doing his job, which felt oppressive in comparison. Mark's paid work and his project with Chris may have looked similar, but Chris's using *Lead with Empathy* imbued their collaboration with MVIP. Mark's bosses could have motivated Mark as Chris did, but they didn't. Almost no one does, so when Chris, or anyone, connects someone's passions to a task, they love working on it. We all do. We love working on what we care about.

Within six months, Chris led his first seminar that brought in over $10,000.

Deepak and the Family Store

Deepak was an NYU student who did these exercises. He was about 20 years old and majoring in political science. After taking my course, he went home for winter vacation. When he returned, he told me that his parents had asked him to make himself useful by working the floor of their retail business, selling antiques.

Deepak had never taken a sales course nor a business course besides mine, so he used all he had—*Meaningful Connection* to connect with customers, then *Make People Feel Understood* to learn their interests, and *Lead with Empathy* to motivate them to buy based on their interests.

The result: He outsold the professional salespeople who had worked the same floor for years.

He told me that *Lead with Empathy* taught him two useful leadership insights through sales. First, you couldn't tell by looking at people what they wanted or were willing to spend. You had to talk to them, and when you did you learned a lot. Second, when you knew what they wanted—their passions—you could connect their passions to things that were open to take on meaning, like antiques. So he did *Lead with Empathy* with customers on the floor; created MVIP for them by showing how an antique for sale met their interests; and made many happy, satisfied customers.

The *Lead with Empathy* Exercise

Make People Feel Understood had you lead people to talk about their passions. You probably had some rewarding conversations where they shared a lot. As much as people like *talking* about their passions, they love *acting* on them.

Connecting someone's passion to your task imbues it with MVIP. Many managers assume others' motivations, don't learn their passions, and motivate them with external incentives. They devalue their passions by valuing external incentives over them, like the old man giving the kids the dollars, only he did it on purpose. Most managers do it like bulls in china shops of people's emotions. We did *Make People Feel Understood* to make people feel comfortable sharing their passions. You probably felt a tug to influence them with what they shared. Once Phil Jackson knew about Shaquille O'Neal's competition with Wilt Chamberlain, he knew he could motivate him with it.

Devaluing people's passions leads them to forget or suppress them, resent their work and managers, and want to leave projects.

Motivating people to resist you and leave the project is the opposite of effective leadership.

Lead with Empathy enables people to work for reasons they wanted to in the first place. They'll often feel liberated, thinking things like, "*Finally,* I can do this for the reasons I wanted to." They'll feel inspired and often work hard. They will often ask you to raise standards, hold them more accountable, give them more responsibility, hold deadlines, and manage them more tightly. They'll thank you for leading them to work so hard.

If you've had a professor for a class you loved (or sports coach, music teacher, manager, etc.), you know the feeling of working hard for yourself, not the professor, even though the professor assigned the work. You felt like you were improving yourself. You appreciated their standards and deadlines for motivating you. You wanted them to evaluate you.

Note that this exercise does not require you to have authority over the people you lead. You can do this exercise with people anywhere in an organization or outside. My students often use it to lead their work managers to manage them how they like. Another application is to motivate clients to buy, like Deepak did. Another is to attract people to your teams and start them on your project. Another is to overcome misunderstandings in personal relationships.

I recommend trying the exercise in a variety of contexts, not just the workplace.

What to Do

Practice the script at least three times in one direction and once in the other. In university, I assign students to do it once a day for a week.

The Script

This exercise sandwiches *Make People Feel Understood* with two steps before and one step after it. The new steps are in bold:

1. **Think of a task you want done that someone you know can do**.
2. **Know that if you lead them to do that task for their passion, they will feel emotional reward.**
3. Ask, "What's your passion?" or something similar, like, "I can tell that you work harder on this than you have to. What's your motivation to care so much?"
4. They'll usually give a cocktail-party answer.
5. Confirm your understanding.
6. *Confirmation/Clarification Cycle*:
    - Let them correct you.
    - Ask confirmation or clarification questions to refine your understanding.
    - Confirm your new understanding.
7. Repeat to *Universal Emotion*.
8. Connect their passion (their *Universal Emotion*) to your task.

Example

Since most of *Lead with Empathy* overlaps with *Make People Feel Understood*, if someone's task was, say, for me to buy his or her leadership book, he or she could have led me through the dialogue in the example in chapter 18 and then added,

> You know, if you want to learn and grow as a leader, I can tell you about a book that covers someone growing a lot like you, with some subtle but important differences. People who have

read it found it helped their development. I think you might like reading it.

And I would feel motivated to buy the book or at least read it.

Discussion

Note that unlike *Make People Feel Understood*, which you can start with anyone, you start *Lead with Empathy* with someone who can do a task you want done. Also, instead of asking for the person's passion broadly, you'll generally ask about his or her passion in terms of how it is relevant to the task. For example, questions like the following show how to lead people to share passions relevant to the task you want done:

> I notice you put more attention into the design when you work on weekly reports. Am I right that you care more about it than most?

or

> You seem to like working on this project. What's your passion behind it?

Step 8 is easier in practice than in the abstract. You generally say in this step that to achieve the person's goal, you think that working on the task could help. If you want someone to finish a report by Friday and the person's Universal Emotion is to make his or her parents proud, you might say, "You know, I don't know your parents personally, but with people depending on this report and the time crunch we're under, I have a feeling that telling them you got it done on time with high quality would make them proud. I'd be happy to help you make that work if you want." It may sound contrived when it's not about your passion, but to someone who just mentioned how much he or she wants to make his or her parents proud, the words give the task meaning.

The first time you *Lead with Empathy*, finding a task appropriate to someone you know may feel hard. By the fifth time, you'll wonder how you led people on important projects without first learning their relevant passions. You deprived them of MVIP if you didn't connect their passions to their work. Students often start practicing *Lead with Empathy* on work-related tasks. You'll find many outside work, like for someone to listen to you, to stop interrupting you, to help you move, to consider your proposal, to help around the house, and so on.

Is *Lead with Empathy* Manipulation?

People often ask if leading people through their emotions is manipulation. Learning experientially helps best here. After you lead a few people this way, you see how much people love and prefer it. Even more, after someone leads you with empathy a few times, you'll see how liberating and comfortable it feels. A few comments may help.

IT PASSES THE GOLDEN RULE

People don't ask if it's manipulation after being led this way themselves. In fact, one of my clients' most common questions after learning to lead this way is how to get their bosses to lead them this way.

When you feel understood on something important and your passion connects to your work, you feel great and often inspired, like, "*Finally*, I can talk about these things I care about" and "*Finally*, I can work for the reasons I've wanted to." When you feel that joy and enthusiasm, you'll wish your leaders led you this way.

If something passes the Golden Rule of reciprocity—that you want someone else to do it unto you—it's hard to label it as bad. More likely, you'll have a problem leading *without* relevant emotions.

A FIRM LEAD HELPS

If you've partner danced, like waltz or tango, you know one person leads and the other follows. The leader pushes the follower to indicate where to move.

Growing up I learned not to push people, so when I learned partner dancing, I led lightly. Then a dance teacher gave an exercise where the women led the men. For the first time I was on the receiving end of a light lead—yuck! How confusing! I couldn't tell what my partner wanted me to do, so I couldn't follow or perform to my ability.

A firm lead, when skillful, helps a lot more than a weak one. When he or she knows what the leader wants, the follower has more freedom to spin and so on, even to disagree or push back. Only when you know someone will catch you will you risk falling.

You can call a firm lead manipulation, but the label doesn't matter. What matters is what builds relationships and works.

YOU'LL DEVELOP MORE EMPATHY FOR THEM

The feeling you'll get when you reach a Universal Emotion of "I bet if I led the person with this, I could get them to do a lot more" may sound like you could abuse it, but "universal" means you also feel that emotion. That's empathy. You will automatically feel like you couldn't and wouldn't use what they shared for your advantage at their expense.

Besides feeling respect for their passion, you also recognize that abusing their trust would undermine that relationship. So, from a rational, pragmatic perspective, you sense that it's not in your interests to take advantage of them.

AFTER PRACTICE, YOU'LL CALL EXTERNAL INCENTIVES MANIPULATIVE

Most people contrast *Leading with Empathy* with what they're used to—usually, leading through external incentives like hiring, promoting, offering raises, increasing responsibility, demoting, and firing. These tools help manage but not necessarily lead.

After leading people based on their emotions, you'll look back on leading people with external incentives as fake and manipulative, and not in the sense of a firm lead in partner dancing. People need to pay rent and eat, so salaries matter, but nobody wants their gravestone to say, "He got the corner office" or "She rose in the organization fast." Neglecting emotions neglects MVIP.

In time, *Lead with Empathy* will lead you to base more and more of your professional and personal relationships. Sadly, our world's focus on external incentives has led many managers to lose sight of what creates MVIP. For better or worse, after people experience you leading them with empathy and MVIP, society's lack of it will drive them back to you.

EXERCISE CHECKLIST

- ❏ Did you think of what task you wanted before starting?
- ❏ Did you do the exercise at least three times?
- ❏ Did you have someone do the script back to you?
- ❏ Did you pay attention to the other person's reaction?
- ❏ Did you pay attention to your reaction?
- ❏ Did you look for ways to improve each time?

Stop reading. Put the book down and do the exercise.

REFLECTION QUESTIONS

I recommend reflecting on your experience with this chapter's exercise before continuing. You can reflect about anything you found relevant, but here are some questions you may want to consider:

- Did you sense the ability to lead people when they shared their motivations?
- Did you sense a shift in focus to people's motivations?
- How did it feel for you to connect someone's passion to your task?
- How did it look to them to have you connect their passion to your task?
- How did they seem to react?
- Where and how might you apply your experience in the rest of your life?

Post-Exercise

Once I made a habit of leading with empathy, compassion, and MVIP, I couldn't think of leading with only external incentives again, which I find superficial, ineffective, and impersonal in comparison. You need external incentives for management, but I distinguish leadership from management. If people don't like sales, a big bonus won't inspire them to like it. But if you connect their passion to a task so that they feel ownership of it, then if the project needs selling, they'll figure it out. They'll probably feel more like they're fulfilling their passion or serving their community, but they'll do it and thank you for enabling them to.

Instead of leading through, say, offering a promotion, *Lead with Empathy* leads you to ask, "What would this promotion mean to this person?" If you don't know the answer, you realize the importance of the Clarification/Confirmation Cycle to find out the people's Universal Emotions and what they care about. When you can answer, you connect their passion to the task and create MVIP for them in their work, which you'll both find rewarding.

Students often start *Lead with Empathy* tentatively. They wonder if they'll be able to motivate others as I described. Some aren't yet comfortable talking about emotions and passions. For many, the first time it clicks is transformational—on a scale that could only have come experientially. It also reveals a path to leading like their heroes and role models. It may take time and practice, and you'll make mistakes, but it's a matter of practice. There are no mysteries or superhuman leaps.

I hope you've seen something similar and feel motivated to keep developing. If you do, the results are a world of difference from people who failed at leadership challenges they were unprepared for and concluded they couldn't lead or weren't born to.

I hope you've also had people do the exercise with you to experience personally the MVIP that *Lead with Empathy* creates in the follower. In my experience, it's liberating, inspiring, and fun.

Inspiring Your Teams and John Wooden

Most leaders would love to do what John Wooden did. Wooden was one of the greatest coaches of any sport in any time. He coached the

UCLA men's basketball team to 10 championships in 12 years, among other achievements. No one has won more than four since. He didn't just coach his players to win. He coached them to become better people.

While books have been written by and about him and his coaching, players he coached describe his practice as having a core like *Lead with Empathy.*

Kareem Abdul-Jabbar was one of his top players, winning three college championships. Despite later winning six NBA championships as a professional with other coaches, he describes Wooden's leadership almost beyond compare:

> It's hard to talk about Coach Wooden simply because he was a complex man, but he taught in a very simple way. He just used sports as a means to teach us how to apply ourselves to any situation. Any success that I've had as a parent, I have to give Coach Wooden credit for showing me how it was done.
>
> He didn't expect much from us. He just wanted us to do what he did, which was to get our education and learn how to compete according to the rules. It made a big difference to us that he never expected us to do anything that he didn't do. But then again he graduated from Purdue on time and was a consensus All-American, so he set quite an example and it made it possible to understand that we could do it, but it took some work and he showed us how to do it.
>
> He was more like a parent than a coach. He was a selfless and giving human being, but he was a disciplinarian. We learned all about those aspects of life that most kids want to skip over. He wouldn't let us do that.

Talk about MVIP: "*Any* success that I've had as a parent, I have to give Coach Wooden credit." Not just success in basketball but *as a parent*, which happened years later. Even with Abdul-Jabbar's passion for basketball, his children must have meant more. That's how much Wooden's leadership meant.

How did Wooden do it? Abdul-Jabbar tells us, "He taught in a very simple way. He just used sports as a means to teach us how to apply ourselves to any situation." Sounds like *Lead with Empathy*—connecting his players' passion (for winning basketball games) to his tasks (of discipline, practice, and what "most kids want to skip over"). Despite having the top recruits in the nation, Wooden began the first practice of each season with exercises as basic as how to put on socks.

His players learned discipline, education, playing by the rules, and all the lofty goals leaders aspire to teach. Discipline, integrity, and such don't come from lectures, nor by listening to others' stories or watching inspirational videos. They come from low-level tasks with quality and attention to detail, like putting on socks when done with passion, which *Lead with Empathy* instills. Academic approaches to teaching leadership teach *about* integrity without necessarily developing it. *Lead with Empathy* develops it without necessarily talking about it.

John Wooden was human. What he did, you can, too. You live in different circumstances, so your outcomes may look different, but you can inspire as effectively with your teammates. The path for you to get those results is the same as the one for his players to get theirs: learn their passions and connect them to the task of practicing the basics.

CHAPTER 20

Inspire

Martin Luther King Jr.'s "I Have a Dream" speech is widely regarded as one of the great acts of leadership by one of history's greatest leaders. If you haven't watched it lately, I recommend it.

What was the point of the "I Have a Dream" speech?

I'm not asking rhetorically. If you've heard the speech, what was its point? If you haven't heard it recently, listen to it again and try to answer the question, what was King's goal? King was a leader, and the speech was a clear act of leadership. He didn't give the speech for his health.

When I ask this question in classes, seminars, and workshops, the room quiets. People look thoughtful. Some struggle. They suggest things like "to raise awareness," "to raise consciousness," or "to inspire people." While the speech does those things, they're vague answers, and effective leaders don't lead vaguely. Do you think he could have written and delivered such a speech thinking, "I want to raise awareness"? King had goals and wanted listeners to play their roles achieving them. He specified those roles in the speech. They were difficult and dangerous roles, but people followed.

Moreover, his structure was the same as *Lead with Empathy*'s. I didn't make up the practice of inspiring people to act by connecting their passion to a task. I identified what worked and created exercises to learn it through practice. King was one of my models and inspirations.

Let's see how he did it.

He started by setting the context and tone—invoking the Gettysburg Address, the Declaration of Independence, the Constitution, and the Emancipation Proclamation, referring to the inequality of the day as a promissory note marked insufficient funds.

The context and tone set, King continued to where he gave specific instruction:

> I am not unmindful that some of you have come here out of great trials and tribulations. Some of you have come fresh from narrow jail cells. And some of you have come from areas where your quest for freedom left you battered by the storms of persecution and staggered by the winds of police brutality. You have been the veterans of creative suffering. Continue to work with the faith that unearned suffering is redemptive. Go back to Mississippi, go back to Alabama, go back to South Carolina, go back to Georgia, go back to Louisiana, go back to the slums and ghettos of our northern cities, knowing that somehow this situation can and will be changed.

Did you see the imperatives? It's the most clear and direct instruction in the speech: *Continue to work. Go back.* Go back for what? To face suffering as continued civil disobedience.

His task for his followers was clear: Knowing the risks, go to Mississippi, Alabama, and the other centers of inequality and face jail, battering, brutality, and other suffering. "Creative suffering" meant beatings, being attacked, and risking being murdered.

Few leaders instruct people to such difficult tasks, but his followers continued to follow him more than ever. Why? People don't risk their lives through being convinced of the logic of nonviolent civil disobedience. Many disagreed that it could work anyway. They did it because he *inspired* them. Leadership rarely means inspiring people to do what *you* want. It means inspiring them to do what *they* want. In Dwight Eisenhower's words, "Leadership is the art of getting someone else to do something you want done because he wants to do it."

To inspire people by connecting their passion to a task, they must believe you understand them. For all of King's challenges, he knew that most listeners felt he understood them. His home had been bombed. Four months earlier, he had been jailed. He still kept working. His "Letter from Birmingham Jail" painfully recounted the personal suffering and inequality he faced and kept working past. He had experienced unearned creative suffering. They knew he understood.

So challenging a task needs a matching passion, which King supplied—his dream—and connected to the task of nonviolent civil disobedience. King concluded his speech with that passion:

> When we allow freedom to ring, when we let it ring from every village and every hamlet, from every state and every city, we will be able to speed up that day when all of God's children, black men and white men, Jews and Gentiles, Protestants and Catholics, will be able to join hands and sing in the words of the old Negro spiritual, "Free at last! Free at last! Thank God Almighty, we are free at last!"

In essence, amid the vibrant imagery, brilliant rhetoric, and everything else that made the speech great, King gave the simple, clear leadership message:

> Create freedom for all by practicing nonviolent civil disobedience in the most risky places.

Millions followed. They may have looked from the outside like they were risking their lives, being blasted by fire hoses, and being jailed, but in their hearts and minds they were creating freedom. They may have looked like they were following his instructions, but inside they were working for themselves—in particular, to becoming free at last.

A task without passion is at best management. Passion without a task is idle dreaming. King imbued their work with meaning, value, importance, and purpose by connecting their passion to an effective task. Nobody wants to go to jail, get attacked by dogs, or risk their lives, but everyone wants freedom.

You may never speak to hundreds of thousands of people and instruct them to risk their lives, but *Lead with Empathy* will still give their work MVIP. Follow the script—behave and communicate so that they feel comfortable sharing their passions with you, make them feel understood (which is different from understanding them), connect their passion to your task—and you will inspire them.

Doing so will also develop your empathy, compassion, listening skills, and so on. Practice *Meaningful Connection*, *Lead with Empathy*, the *Confirmation/Clarification Cycle*, and *Universal Emotion* until you master them, and you will lead as effectively as anyone.

The *Inspire* Exercise

Most students do *Lead with Empathy* tentatively, as if they're walking barefoot in a dark room, afraid to stub their toes. This chapter's exercise, *Inspire*, is to repeat the steps of *Lead with Empathy*. Experience has shown that repeating *Lead with Empathy* leads you to perform it as if you are striding into a bright room, confident of each step. Like any skill, if you rehearse, you get it and it looks effortless. If you don't, you won't.

The confidence comes from seeing people respond enthusiastically and finding meaning in the task. A leader acting assertively, confidently, and empathetically—based on experience, skill, and awareness, not authority, aggression, or entitlement—is easier to follow. Success with *Lead with Empathy* will give you that confidence.

Your teammates will feel inspired when you *Lead with Empathy* with confidence. Inspired people

- ▸ Work harder, more diligently, and longer than uninspired people.
- ▸ Work for internal motivations, emotions, and passions.
- ▸ Feel like they're working for themselves, not someone else.
- ▸ Feel liberated, like, "Finally, I can work for the reasons I always wanted to".
- ▸ Feel deeply thankful to the person who motivated them.
- ▸ Feel the work rewarding in itself.
- ▸ Want to do more when their project finishes.
- ▸ Look back fondly at the amount of work they did.
- ▸ Value missing less-rewarding activities, no matter how fun, not as a sacrifice.
- ▸ Care about quality and make it happen.
- ▸ Put aside distraction to focus on their tasks.
- ▸ Feel like the person who inspired them understands them deeply.
- ▸ Want the person who inspired them to lead them again.

Sounds like how Abdul-Jabbar described playing under Wooden to me.

Mastering Performance

As you *Lead with Empathy*, like an actor rehearsing lines or a musician practicing a piece, the focus of your attention will evolve and your technique will improve. You will go through the following process, the same as a musician, actor, singer, or other performer.

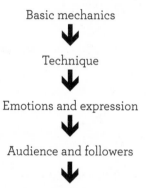

The Evolution of a Performer's Focus

Basic mechanics

Technique

Emotions and expression

Audience and followers

Beyond—revolutionizing or redefining a field

For example, consider someone who wants to learn guitar to become a rock star. First, he needs to learn the instrument and basic chords. He has to focus on where to put his fingers and how to strum. His work is mechanical and hardly related to music. That's all he can do.

After mastering the mechanics, he can focus on following a score. He uses what he mastered in the last stage as the tools for this one but plays without expression. That's all he can do. Many aspiring leaders who only learned to manage are at this stage in their leadership development.

After mastering the score, the guitarist can focus on what he wants to express through the music. He plays with heart. In this stage, he becomes an artist—maybe a studio musician.

He can keep practicing beyond "just" becoming an artist. After mastering expressing himself through the music, he can pay attention to the audience and focus on it. Then he can become a rock star. He uses his tools as an artist, which he can now take for granted, to "play" the audience, as can you as a leader. Martin Luther King Jr. worked at this level, as do movie stars and great sports champions. Effective leaders focus on the people they lead—*their* interests and motivations. The way to get there starts with mastering yourself, practicing, and rehearsing, the same as the guitarist and masters of every other ASEEP field.

When you are confident enough with your delivery that you can take your behavior for granted, you will focus on the people you lead—their words, expressions, meaning, and so on. You did it before when you learned to walk. You had to concentrate on your legs and where to put your feet. You fell many times. The same with learning to talk. You once had to work hard to coordinate moving your lips and tongue. Now you take for granted the most fine-tuned coordination of all the muscles involved in speech. You just speak. You just walk. With practice, soon you'll just lead.

In time you'll feel something missing if you *haven't* first learned how your teammates' relevant passions connect to the team's work, even for people you aren't formally leading.

What to Do

This chapter's exercise is to repeat the steps of *Lead with Empathy* in each direction but with more confidence based on your experience. You will probably also select a more appropriate task and put the other person's interests before yours more effectively.

You can do the exercise with someone new or someone you've worked with already. You can find a new passion to connect with a new task or an existing one.

1. Think of a task you want done that someone you know can do.
2. Know that if you lead them to do that task for their passion, that they will feel reward
3. Ask "What's your passion?" or something similar, like, "I can tell you work harder on this than you have to. What's your motivation to care so much?"
4. They'll usually give a cocktail-party answer.
5. Confirm your understanding.
6. *Confirmation/Clarification Cycle*:
   - Let them correct you.
   - Ask confirmation or clarification questions to refine your understanding.
   - Confirm your new understanding.
7. Repeat to *Universal Emotion*.
8. Connect their passion (their *Universal Emotion*) to your task.

EXERCISE CHECKLIST

- ❑ Did you do the exercise at least once?
- ❑ Did you pay attention to the other person's reaction?
- ❑ Did you pay attention to your reaction?
- ❑ Did you look for ways to improve each time?
- ❑ Did you have someone do the script back to you?

 Stop reading. Put the book down and do the exercise.

REFLECTION QUESTIONS

I recommend reflecting on your experience with this
chapter's exercise before continuing. You can reflect about
anything you found relevant, but here are some questions
you may want to consider:

◆ Did you feel you inspired people?
◆ If not, do you think you could with practice?
◆ How did people you led this way seem to feel?
◆ How did you feel leading them this way?
◆ How do you think your practice and technique will
  change with experience?
◆ Where and how might you apply your experience in
  the rest of your life?

Post-Exercise

Few rewards compare with devoting yourself wholeheartedly and
unreservedly to a task you feel passion for and finishing it. This
chapter's exercise was designed to enable you to lead people to do
that. It's a tremendous gift to give someone that happens to get
your work done, too. The more you give people credit for it, the
more they admire you.

Everyone has passions, even those who hide them. And everyone loves telling their passions to people who support them. *Meaningful Connection* and *Make People Feel Understood* get people to
overcome feelings of vulnerability to share their passions. *Lead
with Empathy* and *Inspire* give people direction to act. You'll find
many people you lead this way never got to act wholeheartedly on
their passions before. Many of them will later speak of you as Abdul-Jabbar spoke of Wooden.

I hope that you reach the level of mastery where you can inspire others predictably and deliberately. As far as I know, it only comes through disciplined, dedicated practice—in the case of leading, *Meaningful Connection*, *Lead with Empathy*, and *Inspire* is a simple path that works. Mastery will make you the leadership equivalent of the rock star musician, champion athlete, inspirational civil rights leader, and commander that soldiers risk their lives for.

Mastery means transitioning you from cautious optimism, wondering if you're manipulating people, to enthusiastically leading them by meaningfully connecting, making them feel understood, connecting their passions to your task, and unleashing them to act on their passions. It means feeling the intimacy, empathy, self-awareness, sensitivity, and compassion that effective leadership and teamwork create—in work teams and in your closest relationships. It means that you won't dream of going back to leading impersonally without knowing people's passions. It means no more pointless conversations about weather, sports, and traffic on the way over. It means seeing leading like Martin Luther King Jr., or whomever are your role models, as a matter of practice and rehearsal, nothing superhuman or that you have to be born with.

The more you practice and hone your skills, the more people will think you were born with them and will call you intuitive or a genius. The irony comes with the territory.

The experience, skills, and beliefs these exercises create will transform your relationships across your life, becoming based in mutual understanding, listening, helping each other, getting things done, and so on. When your teams value their projects, they take responsibility for quality, productivity, and efficiency—more than you could have imposed on them otherwise.

I used to think CEOs said, "Business is about people" so they could pay people less. Now my clients and students tell me that people in their teams contribute more than they could have dreamed of asking them to. In the words of Amy, an MBA and executive,

> I took out an Associate who will be working on my team and
> used your technique. She teared up, saying, no one ever asked
> her these questions and she is so grateful that I am taking an
> approach to her work based on what she likes and wants to do.
> It also revealed some of her deep fears and it was quite
> profound. . . .
>
> Invaluable, thank you. . . . I felt terrific afterward—in that she
> felt great and also that I felt I could get more out of her. She is
> also a friend, so I was conscious that she now reports to me . . .
> but that really was entirely neutralized in this conversation.

This book focuses on leading one-on-one. The same structure of self-awareness, understanding, empathy, compassion, and inspiration by connecting others' passions to your task works with leading many, as King showed. Examples of historic speeches available online that did so include, among many others,

- Martin Luther King Jr.'s "I Have a Dream"
- George Patton's speech to the Third Army
- Oprah Winfrey's Harvard Commencement address
- Susan B. Anthony's account of her addressing the judge who found her guilty of voting as a woman

I leave it as an exercise to the reader to identify in each speech how the leader creates understanding and empathy and what passions he or she connects to which task.

Inspiration alone motivates people to start but doesn't finish the job. Leaders ship, meaning effective leaders see projects to completion, which requires supporting and managing your teams.

CHAPTER 21

Support and Manage

When last we saw Chris the salesman, he turned his frustration with cold calling into a practice of in-person seminars within a few months by leading Mark, an expert in event marketing, to help him. Mark taught Chris everything he knew and helped him market his first event. Still, enthusiasm and even inspiration only got Mark started. I told you the beginning and results but left out the middle, where Chris supported and managed Mark.

"I can't meet for a couple weeks," Mark said to Chris while planning that first event.

"Why not?" Chris asked. The step they were on was easy and didn't need weeks of work.

"I'm not feeling well. I've been putting off my health for a while. I know it's my diet and not exercising. I have to take some time to figure out how to get healthy again," Mark explained.

Years before, Chris had worked as a personal trainer. "Mark, I'm an expert in helping people with health and fitness. I can help you with all that," he said and then described his background and how he could help.

"I can't accept. It's too much," Mark said, probably sensitive to making more money than Chris.

Chris insisted. Mark eventually accepted. Chris and Mark then met a few times to identify Mark's needs, his habits, and his goals and then to develop practices to achieve his goals. In the end, Mark didn't need time off from Chris's project, and their collaboration became two-way. Mark helped Chris with marketing and Chris helped Mark with health and fitness.

A skeptical observer could say Chris was just doing something easy to get more work in less time out of someone already working for free without paying him any more.

This view misses what support means to the person receiving it. If you only look at money, Chris didn't spend any to get more work out of Mark, but Mark already had money. Money from his job was *devaluing* his passion. He was working for Chris for personal reasons his employer missed.

Meanwhile, Mark had been sick enough to put off something he enjoyed. From Mark's perspective, Chris gave him health and enabled him to work on what he cared about, *finally*, as a break from the drudgery of his paid job. Chris freed him from the distraction and helplessness of his deteriorating health. Mark insisted on paying Chris for his time. Chris protested but eventually relented and accepted a token $20.

In other words, technically, Chris got paid to receive world-class training in exchange for helping with some easy (for him) fitness training. From Mark's perspective, he got health, longevity, and a fun project in exchange for helping a friend with some easy (for him) marketing training, too.

Everybody needs support. Leaders who support their teams will create productive and efficient teams with high morale. When you *Lead With Empathy* and *Inspire*, your team will feel like you're supporting their passions, increasing the MVIP you created. They will care less about how easy your job is than how much you helped. Your job often becomes easy and rewarding since so many workers need similar support, which you get good at giving. In Chris's case, supporting Mark was easy and enjoyable, but Mark still appreciated it for the value of his health, not Chris's effort.

Chris and Mark's relationship illustrates a common result of leading and supporting with the exercises from Unit 4. Chris and Mark mutually supported each other. They ended up connecting as friends, not just people doing a transaction. Each gave what he was strong in and got what he was weak in. Each looked forward to working with the other.

The leader and follower roles blur when you *Support and Manage* after you *Lead with Empathy* because each becomes so invested in the projects' success. Each leads when leading helps and follows when following does.

There is one big difference between Chris and Mark in the partnership. Chris initiated it, created Mark's MVIP, and acted on the support Mark needed. From then on, Chris could let their roles evolve based on the project's needs.

Chris's ability to initiate and sustain projects means that his next project will be as rewarding. Mark's next project, if he doesn't have those skills, may or may not be as rewarding. Like others without these skills, he'll likely consider himself lucky if a project is so rewarding for him.

Lead people this way, and they'll want you to lead them again.

The *Support and Manage* Exercise

This exercise is to sit with someone you're leading and recalling his or her passion and the MVIP you created to create a role for you to Support and Manage the person.

What to Do

You've connected a few people's passions to your tasks. Some of the tasks will take time, money, and other resources to complete. If you only *Inspire* people, they'll want to do the task but may lose motivation, run out of resources, or hit other problems that require support.

1. Before meeting, on your own, think of the tasks you are leading people on and put yourself in their places. Write down what they can't provide themselves.
2. Meet one-on-one with each person you are leading.
3. Remind them of your conversations connecting their passion to your task so they feel understood and motivated during this conversation. (Note that their passions may evolve, so be prepared to learn and adjust.)
4. Together, think of what support will make them effective and free them from distraction and what communication and check-ins you'll need. Write these things down together.
5. Figure out what you can and can't do.
6. Create work plans for both of you.
7. Support them according to the plan until the project finishes.

Do this exercise with each person you are leading.

You will often end up telling those you lead, at their request, specifically what to do and having them tell you specifically what they want from you. What would feel like micromanaging if you hadn't connected their passion to the task will feel to someone you inspired like support. They will see you as a resource for acting on their passion. They will often feel grateful for getting to work more. Until you grasp the value of the MVIP you are creating for them, you may not feel you are worth the effort they put in. When you realize that they are working for themselves, you will sense how much they value the work.

When I lead, I think of my support role like the founder's in a startup who takes responsibility for what anyone else doesn't. If the team needs paper clips at 2 a.m. and the only store that's open is across town, the founder gets them. When the team feels that support and it keeps them from losing focus, they give more, even if you aren't burning as many calories or spending as much time on the project.

You can even hire someone to support them, reduce your load, and expand the team's abilities, although you'll still hold ultimate responsibility.

Many students are surprised at the amount of both freedom and control this exercise gives them. For example, when people feel passion for their work, they will often ask you to manage them in ways that would feel like micromanaging otherwise. They'll say things like, "Tell me exactly what to do and how to evaluate my performance so I know how to do it," or "What are all the deadlines and subdeadlines for each part of the project? Who depends on me when?"

Managing people is as important as leading them. People lose focus and meaning in their work without support and management, no matter how inspired they felt at first.

Most of us have felt inspired and worked with effective people without the team reaching its goal. An inspired team needs effective management to support it. Leadership and management overlap significantly but have many distinct parts. Most people have more experience and skills managing.

Common Needs

Here is a partial list of common needs of teams and team members, in no particular order. Different people and teams have different needs. Your communication skills, self-awareness, sensitivity, and experience will guide you to learn the needs of your teams that you can support.

- Material resources (such as money, supplies, food)
- Protection from others wanting their labor and time—"air cover"
- Conflict management
- Connections to others outside the team
- Expectation of success
- Vision
- Feeling understood in their motivation and passion
- Vacations
- Reinspiration
- Motivation
- Standards to meet
- Recognition for their effort
- A shoulder to cry on
- A sense of urgency
- More time
- Less time
- Clarity
- Silence
- Solitude
- Systems (such as computers, schedules)
- Advice
- Space to work
- Material reward
- Nonmaterial reward
- Listening
- Accountability
- Privacy
- A kick in the butt
- Ownership

Doing this exercise with teammates or followers will transition your relationship with them on this project from leading them on this project to managing and supporting them. You generally spend more time managing people than leading them.

If you've led them effectively, they will want to do the work you assigned them for the meaning it brings. Since managing them will feel to them like you are supporting them in their passion, they'll want you to tell them what to do, for example, when appropriate.

By analogy, in a partner dance, for the follower (let's say female) to follow the lead (let's say male), she wants to know that he will support her. He, in turn, needs to know from her what support she will need in order to give it to her. The more they communicate their expectations during rehearsals, the better they both can perform. When she knows he will support her, she can perform to her potential—she can risk falling and experimenting when she knows he will catch her.

How Inspirational Leadership Transforms People You Lead

BEFORE INSPIRATIONAL LEADERSHIP	AFTER
Their labor	A chance to act on what they care about
Responsibility	Ownership
Accountability	Goals
Standards	Direction
Sacrifice	Investment and learning to act on values
Deadlines	Challenges to test their mettle
Time wasters (such as Facebook)	Distractions they want to get rid of
External incentives	Nice to have
Internal motivations	Meaning, value, importance, purpose
You	Inspirer and liberator
Them	Part of a greater cause

EXERCISE CHECKLIST

- ❏ Did you do the exercise at least twice?
- ❏ Did you collaborate to foresee as many needs as possible?

❑ Did you remember that they are doing your work for their reasons, not yours?
❑ Did you create clear tasks for each of you?
❑ Did you clearly state the deliverables and schedules for each of you?
❑ Did you list the resources they need and when?

 Stop reading. Put the book down and do the exercise.

REFLECTION QUESTIONS

I recommend reflecting on your experience with this chapter's exercise before continuing. You can reflect about anything you found relevant, but here are some questions you may want to consider:

◆ How did you feel preparing to talk to others about supporting them?
◆ How did your conversations feel to you?
◆ How did they seem to like the conversations?
◆ Did you get to more or less detail than you expected?
◆ How did the process of transitioning to management compare with how you set up management relationships before?
◆ How did the support and management relationship go following the first conversation?
◆ Where and how might you apply your experience in the rest of your life?

Post-Exercise

In this exercise, did you find yourself telling people what to do, assigning accountability—what used to feel like micromanaging—and seeing them appreciate you for it?

Most people who learned more about management than leadership are surprised by how much their teammates want and welcome specific, detailed instruction—that is, to understand their motivations and connect them to the task.

That emotional connection between teammates and their task gives them ownership and meaning in their work. They want to do it for their own reasons. Without it, management often sounds like, "Here's what the team needs done, here's your role, do your best, I'll hold you accountable." We don't want to sound authoritarian or micromanage, but it's hard to avoid when the people you're leading don't have emotional connections, feelings of ownership, and meaning in their work.

When you *Lead With Empathy* and *Inspire*, you become a resource for them, someone to help them, like a dance follower wants her lead to lead her so that she can do more than she could alone. For a skillful leader, the more clear and firm the lead, the more freedom the person being led has to shine, take more risk, and so on.

The challenge for leading clearly and firmly is to do not too much, not too little, and not too different from what your team needs. The way to find that balance is to know people's passions and motivations. They know their interests and limitations better than you. Unit 4's exercises are designed to develop the compassion, empathy, beliefs, and skills to have them share them with you. When you *Support and Manage,* you match their abilities and interests to the job's needs.

The next stage in leading people is more detailed management, for which many resources exist.

The next stage in your leadership development is to practice the skills and beliefs you developed in this book. Now that you have technique, it's a matter of practice.

Lead people this way—with empathy, compassion, passion, and inspiration to create passion, meaning, value, importance, and purpose—and people will want you to lead them again.

CHAPTER 22

Next Steps

I had three top goals in compiling these exercises.

The first was to enable and empower you—to give you, through doing the exercises, an integrated, comprehensive foundation in the skills, beliefs, and experiences of effective leadership, to lead yourself and others based on understanding yourself and others.

I designed the progression to enable you to create MVIP and passion in yourself, your teams, and your communities, so others feel gratitude to you for leading them to do so much, even to work so hard when necessary, because they'll feel they did it for themselves.

I designed the progression to help you to develop the skills of empathy, compassion, self-awareness, sensitivity, integrity, discipline, and so on essential to effective leadership. I call these things skills because the more you practice them, the more you master them. If you don't practice, they seem unattainable. People without empathy and self-awareness wonder what they mean. No amount of words will explain them. With some practice you start getting them. Practice the right exercises enough and you master them.

My second goal was to create the expectation that what skills, beliefs, and experiences you want, you can develop. If you see someone else lead or do something you can't, know that you need only find out how they got it, make an exercise of it, and do it until you have their skills, beliefs, and experiences—that is, do *The Method*.

To the common question "Are leaders born or made?" I created these exercises to tell you that all great leaders became great through practice. None were born leading. The only limit to your leadership is how much you practice.

My second goal, in other words, was to instill in you one of the most motivational, life-affirming, and empowering beliefs I've had: "What anyone else can do, I can too."

My third goal was to motivate you to find in leading the deep reward, MVIP, and passion that I do, and that it creates the most meaningful, valuable, important, purposeful, and passionate relationships. If so, you'll feel the enthusiasm I do to take on ever more meaningful, valuable, important, and purposeful challenges. Our world has plenty.

If you did the exercises, you know the reward and emotions they create better than I can say, which is the point of Method Learning. If you didn't, go back and do them to find out. Either way,

Practice, practice, practice.

Index